PRISON PARADOX

*When life locks you down,
look to the One who holds the key!*

Jason H. Wiersma

Psalm40 Publishing

PRISON PARADOX
Published by Psalm40 Publishing
PO Box 23
Canton, South Dakota, 57013 USA

Edited by Loretta Sorensen, Prairie Hearth Publishing, LLC
Artwork for the book was developed by:
Travis Lone Hill and Lisa Sasker

Names of any former or current inmates referred to in this content have been changed.

ISBN 978-0-578-54594-3

Printed in the United States of America
First Edition 2019

CONTACT US (or to order more books)
Website: www.psalm40publishing.com
Facebook: Prison Paradox
Or write us:
Prison Paradox
PO Box 23
Canton, SD 57103

*This book is dedicated
to my dad, who taught me
to live life to the fullest,
against the odds.*

Gerald Wiersma, 1951–2018

FOREWORD

The first time I heard about a guy named Jason Wiersma was the night his wife, Ruth, called our house. Ruth had reached out to us because my husband and I helped lead a spiritual retreat in western Iowa. Ruth's husband was coming to that retreat, but she wasn't quite sure how he'd do, given his anxiety and his discomfort in social situations.

We promised to pray, and pray we did.

Jason went to the retreat, and what happened next bears striking similarity to what would happen if you threw a lit match into a fireworks store.

All these years later, if there were a dictionary entry for "On Fire for Jesus," there should be a picture of Jason next to it.

So, when Jason asked me to write the foreword for his forthcoming book, I gave my wholehearted yes. I couldn't wait to read his words and offer my endorsement of his work.

Jason and his wife have become dear friends to us. My husband and I have had the privilege of watching what happens when that spiritual fire stays ablaze. Jason and Ruth have touched countless lives, including ours, with their ministry, wisdom, service, and prophetic vision for the future.

Yet, even though they had become dear to us, there were parts of Jason's story that I had never heard before. Jason's story is nothing short of amazing and compelling, and I loved it so much that I read it in one sitting. (And that's coming from a self-proclaimed book snob.) This page-turner made me think, made me laugh, and made me feel that inner sense of conviction that comes when the Holy Spirit gets under your skin.

I'd love to give you a list of bullet-pointed highlights, but this is a story that needs to unfold for you, as you turn the pages of *"Prison Paradox."*

However, I would be doing an incredible disservice to the message of this book if my foreword dwelt too long on Jason's personal "rebel to redemption" story. His journey is remarkable, to be sure, but this isn't a book primarily about Jason's journey. It's a bold invitation into your own.

Will you say yes to this invitation? I hope you will.

This book will challenge you, push you, and compel you to ask some important questions about the prisons you've been in. And, if we're honest with ourselves, we've all been in prisons—prisons of regret, unforgiveness, shame, and sin.

Jason knows what a prison is like. He spends his days working as a pastor inside the Mike Durfee State Prison. But this book isn't just for men or women living in literal prisons, behind literal bars.

It's for all of us.

As you begin this journey, take a moment to ask God to reveal to you the prisons he's released you from. And then take a moment to consider the prisons that still hold you captive.

If you sense that there are areas where you aren't walking in full freedom right now, Jason has good news for you: the prison cell isn't locked. Jesus turned the key, has swung open the door, and is inviting you to step into freedom.

Nothing disqualifies you from this freedom.

Not your checkered past.

Not your self-doubts.

Not your intellect.

Not your rebel status.

Not your struggle with anxiety or fear.

If you sat across from Jason in his office at the prison, he would tell you, "It's never too late to make the next right decision."

Will you make it?

Maybe, you've already taken those steps. Maybe you've been following the Lord for a while now, and you are living in the full freedom afforded to you. Jason and I celebrate with you! But we want you to know: This book is also for you.

If you sat across from Jason in his office at the prison, he would have something to tell you as well: "Your past is someone's present." Someone, right now, is struggling with the very thing that held you in chains for so long. If that's you, consider sharing this book as a tool to help others who need to find the freedom you've found. Prayerfully consider using this book for group study in your Sunday school class, your prayer group, or your family. Or simply read it as a way to stoke the flames of your own spiritual fire.

This is a book about freedom. It's a book about grace. It's a book about God's unending love for you. I'm profoundly honored to join Jason in inviting you along for the journey.

My prayer is that when you reach the last page, you will stand up, with your face tipped to heaven and say:

Here I am, Lord. Send me.

— Jennifer Dukes Lee, author of *It's All Under Control,*
The Happiness Dare, and *Love Idol*

CONTENTS

INTRODUCTION

I must be honest right from the start. The title of this book is a tad misleading. Although I have, at this point in my life, 12 years of prison experience, most of that has been as a prison pastor. I've never actually lived in a physical prison.

A prison can be defined as a building in which people are legally held as a punishment for a crime they committed or while awaiting trial. Although I have many friends who are incarcerated, I've never spent a night in a literal prison.

But I have been imprisoned, held captive by multiple things during my life. I would say some of my own personal prisons tormented me worse than perhaps an incarceration behind bars and a razor-wire fence would have.

The *Prison Paradox* is that, although many people never get incarcerated in a physical sense, I believe everyone has been imprisoned by something at some point. There are physical prisons, spiritual prisons and mental prisons (amongst others).

The worst part about being held captive is that we can, at times, create a prison of our own making based on falsehoods we've believed. It's likely we don't even realize we live in it.

To illustrate what I'm talking about, I'd like to tell you about a horse I once met. Years ago, I enjoyed buying horses that were rough in either body condition or attitude, and giving them the food and/or training needed to improve their value. One day, I responded to an ad that offered some horses for sale in my area. The bloodlines were precisely what I preferred.

My friend Dan and I went to the farm to look at the animals.

I was greatly dismayed to see horses housed in yards and buildings in a very dilapidated condition. The general condition of the animals was not good, either. Asking prices for the horses were unreasonable, considering their current situation. But my heart wouldn't allow me to leave without rescuing some of them from their state of despair.

One horse in particular stands out in my memory. She was a seven-year-old beautiful dun mare penned up all alone in a dark corner of a rickety barn. Her owners had never cleaned her pen, just added straw. For seven years she walked on literally feet of manure and bedding. She constantly ducked so her head wouldn't hit the rafters above. Her feet had never been trimmed and looked more like skis than hooves.

I decided to rescue her, paying $700 to get her out of that dark corner. The crazy thing was, when we opened the stall gate and tried to get her out, she didn't want to go! Why?

You see, she was born in that stall and over the next seven years never left it. She knew no other life. It's a sad thing to see a captive that doesn't even realize the benefits of freedom. Even more sad when it's a person rather than an animal.

Eventually, I was able to coax the mare out of the barn. I trimmed her hooves and she adjusted to living in a pasture with other horses. I kept her a few years before selling her. Last I heard she was frolicking somewhere in the green grasses of Kentucky.

Imagine if she had never left that pen. She would never have experienced a refreshing rain, the feel of the sun on her back, the comfort of being part of a herd. Simply put, she would have missed out on life.

I'm not sure what kind of memory a horse might have, but I would bet we would have had a really hard time putting her back into that stall after she tasted freedom.

Sadly, it's not just horses that can miss out on the benefits of freedom.

I've met many people who are stuck in their own private prison. I know what that feels like because I've been among them. In this book, I share some seasons of my own journey to freedom as well as stories from both incarcerated and free people alike that will help identify some of the things that can imprison us.

Fact is, I would say, many inmates in my prison congregation have more freedom than many people on the "outs."

Another "prison paradox" is that good can come out of a person being sent behind the razor wire fence. That may seem to be a contradictory statement, but after reading this book I think you'll agree that it's true.

My hope is that, as you read, you will celebrate with me the freedom found in Jesus Christ. If you are currently stuck in your own private prison, I pray this book will help you, like the dun mare, walk through the "barn gate" and into the freedom you've been longing for. Perhaps a freedom you didn't even know existed.

*"Failure is a detour,
not a dead-end street."*

— Zig Ziglar

1

THE PRISON OF
LOW SELF-WORTH

My mom (who taught preschool for many years) came home from a seminar one day and declared to 19-year-old me: "I know what's wrong with you!"

Now that statement gets a person's attention! Answers to my life struggles literally hung on her next words.

Was I dropped on my head when I was a kid?

Was it the lead paint on my bedroom wall?

Did I get switched at birth?

What was wrong with me?

You see, all my life I had dealt with troubling social issues. Sure, I had friends, but sometimes even they turned on me because, well, I was different. I marched to the beat of my own drum, which no one else seemed to hear. If they had, they probably wouldn't have chosen to march with me anyway.

My first experience with school was quite positive. I got

through preschool without much trouble (probably because of all the activities).

But with the more structured kindergarten year, I was like a tomcat hanging out at a dog show. I wasn't fitting in and a lot of barking† came my way.

Sitting still has never been my thing. In fact, I squirmed so much during lunch the teacher put newspapers under my chair to make the subsequent cleanup easier.

I always found things around me that were far more interesting than whatever the lady in front of the classroom was saying. To make matters worse, at times my bad behavior caused me to be confined to the classroom during recess. Recess was my reprieve from the utterly impossible task of keeping my behavior in check within that stuffy little classroom.

I'll always remember my kindergarten teacher's words: "You're not living up to the glowing reports I received from your preschool teacher." I felt the razor wire-fenced prison of shame and low self-worth encircling me.

Other kids jumped at an opportunity to help build those walls. "You're the poster child for abortion," one older girl said. Other actions and words communicated that I was simply a "less than a person" who would never amount to anything. Sadly, I bought into those lies.

While this theme continued during my elementary and middle school years, some teachers, especially gifted with

† What? You never heard a teacher bark?

patience, will always remain dear to my heart. Some friends did, for the most part, accept me for who I was.

Still, my overarching feeling was that whatever was wrong with me would surely put any kind of lasting success out of reach.

In Pastor Jim Logan's book, *Reclaiming Surrendered Ground*, he says this about the voices that influence us: "Each of us has within him a belief system that is the product of these influences —family, education, media, peers, music, etc. I am not suggesting by any means that everything we receive through these sources is false. Not at all. However, our false perceptions based on these influences must be replaced by a belief system based on truth if our behavior is to be acceptable to God."

Many voices around us can beat us to a pulp and imprison us if we let them. The Christian group, Casting Crowns, sings a song that says, "the voice of truth tells me a different story, the voice of truth says do not be afraid." Words are a powerful force that can either drive a person to believe truth or stumble down a spiraling staircase of lies.

It's a proven fact that inmates who leave prison and regularly attend church have far lesser chance of being incarcerated again. Why? Because they consistently hear truth! And if truth is not at the forefront of their minds, lies WILL take over and drag them under, again.

The Word of God is a powerful tool against the father of lies, the devil (John 8:44). As it pertains to my own self-worth,

I like what King David said in Psalm 139:13-14. *"For you formed my inward parts; you knitted me together in my mother's womb. I praise you, for I am fearfully and wonderfully made. Wonderful are your works; my soul knows it very well."*

I don't think there would have been a time in my life I would have denied that I had been knit together in my mother's womb by God. But I had a sense that maybe God handed someone else the needles for a bit, someone who didn't have steady hands, and that messed up the final product, made it unusable.

Many men I've ministered to at Living Stone Prison Church have very low self-esteem and have never considered themselves as being fearfully and wonderfully made. One that comes to mind is a man I'll call Frank. I met him when I was in my 20s and employed as a corrections officer at the South Dakota State Penitentiary. Frank was serving a life sentence for multiple felonies.

I can't begin to imagine the voices that influenced Frank to do the things that led him to prison. Each time I came through the cell hall where he lived, I noticed he struggled, still influenced by voices cutting him down.

Frank was comfortable talking to me. He often complained that rumors about him were circulating through the prison. Careless words were still dictating what he saw as the sum of his own personal value.

Eventually, Frank became suicidal. He was transferred out of the general population into an area where he could be closely watched. Twice I escorted him to the hospital because of self-inflicted injuries. Each time he pulled through.

I wasn't a pastor at that time, but I cared about Frank and told him he was far too valuable to throw himself away. Shortly before I left my job at the prison for a self-employment opportunity, Frank stopped me as I passed his cell.

"Wiersma," he said, "I did something very important yesterday. I surrendered to Jesus."

I immediately expressed my approval of Frank's decision, but wondered if he just told me something that he knew I wanted to hear. Could such a tortured man experience the true transformation he so desperately needed? (My own faith wasn't very mature at that time.)

For all of us, time is the ultimate test as it pertains to our authentic commitment to the Savior. As it turns out, when the Lord brought me back into South Dakota's Mike Durfee State Penitentiary (MDSP) in the role of pastor, I could see Frank's transformation was the real deal. When I ran into him, his appearance had drastically changed. Physically he looked much the same, a little older. But his facial expression revealed peace.

In conversations with Frank, I learned that, beginning with the day of his surrender, the Lord steadily led him out of his place of despair. The voice of the Good Shepherd, Jesus, (John 10:11) overpowered the voices of destruction and low self-worth.

Despite the brokenness of his past life and things he perceived about himself to be wrong, Frank now lives a life of purpose and fulfillment. He will live out his physical life in the confines of a prison, but he escaped the mental prison of seeing himself as having no value.

In regard to my own low self-worth prison, when Mom said she knew what was wrong with me, it was the early 1990s. The Attention Hyperactive Deficit Disorder (ADHD) diagnosis had just emerged.† When Mom heard about it at her seminar, she believed the speaker had described me to a "T."

Before hearing of ADHD, I thought I couldn't concentrate on what people were telling me because I just wasn't intelligent. Frustrated teachers declared me to be lazy.

After hearing about ADHD, I struggled to understand how I should respond to the diagnosis. I read various books on the topic, eventually trying different medications, most of which had undesired side effects.

Over time, I realized God's plan for me included ADHD. I recently saw a sign in a classroom that said: "ADHD isn't something in your child that needs to be fixed. It's a superpower they just need to be taught how to use."

I still struggle to concentrate and am not detail oriented. I could grieve over things I wish I could do better, but I've chosen to embrace the "superpowers."

God has used many of my ADHD traits—such as creativity and a willingness to take Holy Spirit-inspired risks, using them for His glory. There are some things I wouldn't be able

† In my childhood days ADHD was simply called that stupid kid that can't sit down or zip his lips.

to do without my unique personality traits. I will never be a conventional thinker, and I've learned to be thankful for that.

I have found an escape from my own low self-worth prison and learned to listen to the same voice that freed Frank (see more details in subsequent chapters).

The voice of truth has influenced my life story in ways I never believed were possible. God has used me in spite of my weaknesses, giving evidence of how His power works in and through us. Not only has God applied value to my life, in the face of my challenges, He has used my past to encourage people in the present.

A few years ago, my cousin, an elementary teacher at the school I attended, invited me to speak at one of their chapel services. Honestly, I accepted the opportunity with many reservations. Even though decades had passed since I competed my education there, the building provoked vivid, painful memories of unsuccessfully struggling to fit in.

The day I spoke, I was led to be real about the hurt I experienced during my school years. I talked honestly about my struggles with ADHD. I also spoke of God's power to use each of those precious students who listened, whether they were naturally "A" students or struggled just to obtain a "C."

While it seemed that I did the right thing that day, I had a few doubts. However, in the following days, I received letters from some of the students with questions and comments about what I had said. One little boy's mother contacted me, too. He was having the exact problems I had experienced at his age.

I assured the mother of her son's value and his potential to accomplish great things for God and others despite or even because of his weakness (2 Corinthians 12:9).

You see, our past is someone's present. When we have experienced God's blessing through a difficulty, the best thing we can do for fellow strugglers is to point them towards the exit of their self-imposed prison.

Reflection Questions

- Have you ever experienced the prison of low self-worth? If so, what voices were you listening to at the time? (It could be in the present.)
- What does it mean that we are fearfully and wonderfully made?
- What difficulty from your past could be used by God to help someone in the present?
- What would you say is your greatest weakness? Is there a "superpower" within that weakness? If so, how are you or how could you be using it?

"For there is no one so great or mighty that he can avoid the misery that will rise up against him when he resists and strives against God."

— John Calvin

2

THE PRISON
OF REBELLION

Have you ever traded one bad thing for another? Perhaps you swapped a car that got poor gas mileage for one that breaks down often. Either way, it's going to cost you!

Well, eventually I got sick and tired of just being the dumb kid who couldn't sit down and shut his mouth.

I recall times when I sincerely attempted to apply myself to my schoolwork. But I always ended up stressed out and frustrated at how difficult it was. In the end, I gave up.

I distinctly remember when I began getting in trouble in Middle School. At first, I feared the consequences, but over time those feelings started wearing off.

As I moved into my high school years, I fully traded one bad thing for another. I exchanged my role as a class misfit for a rebel tag. At this point, I began learning more about my addictive personality. In my early years, this showed up in my "all in" approach to any hobby or infatuation that could distract me from my pain. Things like Transformer toys and baseball cards dominated my thoughts and time.

As a freshman in high school, I became utterly fascinated with smoking cigarettes. My goal was to try every brand I could and take note of the nicotine high to decide which one was the best. Smoking in school was the ultimate thrill.

When I † eluded staff and got away with smoking, adrenaline kicked in. That led to another addiction: adrenaline junkie. The day I turned 16, I attended a party and got drunk. I remember jumping into my car and driving with blurry vision to the local dance hall.

That night, my parents had given me a reasonable curfew. But I called them, lying about being at a friend's house and staying overnight. They investigated and caught me in my lie. Grounded!

That first drunken escapade gave birth to hundreds more as my lust for alcohol consumed me. I loved the escape booze gave me from my low self-worth prison.

The Bible warns us not to gaze at sparkling red wine that goes down smoothly, lest it bite you like a serpent and cause perversion of the heart (Proverbs 23:31-33). I must have put my own spin on those verses, because I never stopped to stare at the excess of beer and other alcohol products I steadily

---

†   Notice Seth and Wally that, in this book, I didn't narc you out for smoking with me.

poured into my stomach. It never occurred to me that I was poisoning both my mind and my heart.

For me, alcohol brought temporary release from pain. When the drunkenness wore off, I found my prison was even worse. Alcohol didn't change my reality for the better. It just altered it, giving me a false sense of invisibility.

In high school, I learned I could take a punch rather well and started fighting. I "booze cruised" with a friend who sometimes drove his car down the railroad tracks. Intentionally driving into ditches, he loved scaring passengers by whipping out just before bridges and other obstacles to veer back onto the road.

By all rights, other than the Grace of God, I shouldn't have lived to see my 20s. Paving my way with poor decisions, I was on my way to an early grave. Now I realize I could have unwittingly taken others with me.

At the time, high school was a joke. I had already learned that being a good student wasn't possible for me. I invested no legitimate effort in my studies.

I recall the semester when my GPA (grade point average) was in the .90 range. That same semester my irreverent behavior led my Christian school's Bible teacher to send me to the principal's office. The situation sparked a great anger in me. I threw my books into the trash and stomped out.

In my junior year, they suspended me. I vividly recall jumping into my Pontiac Trans Am, roaring out into the street in front of the school and burning rubber in circles. We called them donuts. Study hall students cheered me on.

Finally, I was somebody! I was the class rebel. At the time, it felt good.

By my senior year, I had failed so many classes only a jam-packed schedule would have made it possible for me to grad-uate. Far too hectic for a stupid kid who couldn't sit down and shut his mouth. So, I didn't return to get a diploma.

If you're reading this from the walls of a prison, my rebel-lious behavior may seem pretty pale compared to your own experience. You may be right.

But Jesus also said that from those to whom much is given, much is expected (Luke 12:48). My loving parents raised me to attend church. My life had structure and order. I had exam-ples and guidance that should have caused me to know better. But for a time, I rejected it all to try things my way.

Oxford dictionary defines the word rebellion as "an act of violent or open resistance to an established government or ruler."

My rebellion was against every authority of man and, worse yet, it was rebellion against God. I would never have vocally denied my identity with the Savior, but my actions did. Looking back, I don't condone the things I did, but I've come to understand that God can and does redeem and use broken things. Broken people.

Having been a rebel, I have some "street cred"† with those

† An identifying characteristic by which a person is admired—good, bad or otherwise.

in my congregation who have resisted governing authorities to the point of incarceration. Romans 13:1-2 says: *"Let every person be subject to the governing authorities. For there is no authority except from God, and those that exist have been instituted by God. Therefore, whoever resists the authorities resists what God has appointed, and those who resist will incur judgment."*

This is a hard scripture for us rebels. It points out that rebellion against those in charge and rebellion against God are not separate issues. They're the result of the same problem: an unyielded heart.

As I wrote this, I was on sabbatical, staying at a halfway house in Missouri. Some find it humorous that I took a break from the prison and hung out with parolees instead. (Ok, so that is a little strange.) But it was educational for me.

One of the men at the house was a heavily tattooed, rough looking man by the name of Jake. He had just completed a 20-year sentence and had only been out for 15 days.

I learned that Jake was from the inner city of St. Louis, where his street name was "Suicide." He didn't fear death as he carried out violent tasks on the streets of that city.

One day, I sat down with Jake for coffee and conversation. I casually asked what he wanted out of life over the next five years. A straight shooter, Jake gave me his honest answer: "I don't know for sure."

Jake thought he might follow the Lord and try a different path than he had ever known. Or, go back to running drugs and guns, robbing banks and being a big man on the streets.

I appreciated his honesty and admired the fact that he recognized the difference between the two lifestyles.

In that moment I was able to counsel him on which path to choose. I hope and pray Jake lets the Holy Spirit lead him away from the broad road of destruction and down the narrow path that leads to life (Matthew 7:13-14).

While Jake's early life was steeped in rebellion, I wanted him to know he didn't have to continue that pattern. I pressed him hard on the issue of which path he would choose. To help illustrate my point, I shared my horse story (from the introduction), the mare that had never left the pen where she was born. Jake admitted it was so hard to envision a life fully surrendered to Jesus because it meant taking a journey into the unknown. A path bent on destruction was at least familiar and somewhat predictable.

Jake experienced release from a physical prison. Now he had to take steps to get out of the prison of rebellion and addiction. A hard choice for many and impossible on our own. But, as you'll read in coming chapters, God makes it possible (Luke 18:27, more on that later).

At that same halfway house, I met Doug. He'd been out of prison for quite a while and told me what God had done for him. In high school, he was a phenomenal football player, earning a football scholarship at Penn State. Unfortunately, before arriving at college, his decisions took him to a different kind of "Pen," a penitentiary.

In prison, Doug joined a white supremacist group. Raised

by his grandfather, Doug was taught to believe Caucasians were superior to other ethnic groups. Every other race, he believed, was to be shunned and mistreated.

Because of his radical approach, Doug was stabbed multiple times in gang fights. Somehow, someone always protected him from a tragic demise.

"I tried everything in my own power to find a way out of the pit," Doug told me. "Finally, I found my release in a relationship with Jesus Christ."

Now, Doug speaks to youth groups in diverse school systems about the horrible misconceptions and dangers of racism.

"If I can save one kid from taking the path I went down, I'll have served my purpose," Doug says.

In ministering to inmates, one my favorite phrases is, "It's never too late to make the next right decision."

My congregation is made up of rebels of many kinds: former pagan worshipers, guys who were street thugs, drug dealers, sex addicts and sticky-fingered thieves, even murderers. The beauty of this group is that many of these men, with all kinds of different addictions and rebellions, found the next right decision for them was repentance, turning away from their sin. Turning to God brings pardon from the prison of rebellion through the Grace of God by way of the cross of Jesus Christ.

The cross is the starting point for rebel forgiveness. In most cases, it takes time for an addict to move entirely out of their personal pit. The key is to stay focused on Jesus (Hebrews 12:1-2).

Repentance is sometimes viewed as a New Testament experience. But it pops up in the Old Testament as well. For instance, when the Lord spoke to Solomon, He revealed what to do when Israel found themselves in trouble: *"If my people who are called by my name, humble themselves, and pray and seek my face and turn from their wicked ways, then I will hear from heaven and will forgive their sin and heal their land* (2 Chronicles 7:14)."

Jesus came into this world to bring healing for brokenness. He can heal a "land" and He can heal a life. But repentance is not something He will do for us. The ball is in our court. We must approach Him humbly and turn from rebelling against Him.

I've lost track of the number of people I've personally witnessed cry out to God out of despair brought on by sin. Once they did, they found forgiveness, mercy, and healing. It's not just in others that I've witnessed this process. I've experienced it myself.

I thought I knew what I wanted in life. I believed rebellion and addiction would always be a driving force in my existence. God had an entirely different plan. I learned that the ticket to the adventure of following Jesus is repentance and surrender. In the next chapter, I'll share what led me to that truth.

Reflection Questions

- Do you think low self-worth and rebellion often go together? Why or why not?
- Why is it so hard for some people to break a pattern of rebellion?
- Why have some churches quit teaching about repentance when the Bible is so clear on it?
- "It's never too late to make the next right decision." Do you agree with this statement? How could you apply that thinking to your life?

*"The more we let God take us over,
the more truly ourselves we become
—because He made us. He invented us.
He invented all the different people
that you and I were intended to be . . .
It is when I turn to Christ, when
I give up myself to His personality,
that I first begin to have a real
personality of my own."*

— C.S. Lewis

3

THE GREAT ESCAPE

People love a good escape story. Case in point, the 1994 movie *Shawshank Redemption* is considered to be one of the best motion pictures of all-time. It's the story of Andy Dufresne, who was falsely accused of murder and sent to Shawshank penitentiary, only to elaborately escape years later.

At the top of the original movie poster were the words, "Fear can hold you prisoner, hope can set you free." Millions of viewers have cheered Andy on as he crawled through the sewer pipes of the prison to sweet freedom.

Why so many of us choose to crawl through the sewer (the unpleasantries of life) before we grasp onto the freedom that is offered in Christ is beyond me. After spending my teenage years imprisoned by a life of rebellion, apart from God's will, I experienced a turning point shortly before my 20s. Here's my personal escape story.

If my life was a movie,† there's one scene that would have to be included. The setting was a local pond where my buddy Rob and I were fishing. Two local farm girls came walking by, stopping briefly to chat with us before going on their way.

As they walked away, a new realization started inside me. The girls were good, wholesome, rural Iowa girls, the type any man would be fortunate to marry. I recognized that no girl of that caliber would be interested in a young man in my current state.

I pondered my rebellion and the way I was living. Then, I did something symbolic: I threw my pack of cigarettes into the pond (much to Rob's confusion). As they sank to the bottom, a new season in my life was birthed. It all started with an understanding that I was headed down a path that would lead me to a place I didn't want to go.

That day I quit smoking. I started running and watching what I ate (things I still do today). I was significantly overweight then, but the pounds began falling off. Although it took time to alleviate my problem, I began denying myself the urge to binge drink. It was another step in the right direction for my entire well-being.

These physical improvements were a good and necessary thing for the outside of me, but something far more important was going on inside. I began reading my Bible, so I could

---

†   I've been told I look like Alex Kendrick (multiple times), so I think he'd be the one to play me. ☺

understand for myself all these things I'd been taught since I was a little boy.

As these changes took hold of me, I vividly recall the night I walked in a field near my parent's farm. While enjoying the fresh air and gazing at the night sky, something profound struck me. No, it wasn't a lightning bolt, (deserved as it might have been).

Flooding over me was an overwhelming desire to surrender to the God I'd heard so much about but never really knew. I found myself kneeling on the ground in repentance. Instead of a lightning bolt, I received the gift of God's Grace through Jesus Christ. I had been pardoned of my rebellion and set free to a new life I could never have imagined.

Of all the seasons in my life, this one was the most important. That's because my eternal destination was now made sure. My life's focus has been permanently altered.

It's by the power of the cross that the rest of my story became possible. 2 Corinthians 5:21 is a profound little verse that describes what happens when we come to Jesus. *"For our sake he made him to be sin who knew no sin, so that in him we might become the righteousness of God."*

The incredible truth of the matter is that, when the sinless Jesus went to that cross, He took all our sin upon Himself and His righteousness falls on those who did/would believe in Him.

We are all sinners. You may be reading this and thinking Jason was a real nasty dude back in the day. Or you might be reading this and thinking your sin dwarfs mine.

But, at the foot of the cross, none of that matters. When I made peace with God through Jesus, that meant it was as if Jesus was there destroying property, stealing from stores, drinking and driving (I'll stop—you get the point). But of course, He never did any one of those things. Jesus took my sin upon Himself anyway, as if He had.

And although I should be condemned for my atrocities, instead I am forgiven because my Savior took my place. When God the Father looks at me, instead of my sin stains, He sees the righteousness of Jesus. I can now live in relationship with Him while looking forward to eternity in Heaven.

Fear can hold you prisoner. Hope can set you free. There is no greater fear than living one's life apart from God's Grace. There is no greater hope than a relationship with the Savior who took our death upon Himself so we might live. Praise God for the great escape offered through the cross!

Jesus talked about those who have been forgiven much having much love for Him (Luke 7:47). With that in mind, I work with many men who have much love in their hearts for Jesus, for they understand what they've been delivered from. In fact, for one man named Chris, it's as if Jesus committed murder, attempted another one and was convicted (consider again 2 Corinthians 5:21) while Chris has been miraculously freed.

In his early life, Chris was full of rebellion, sin and addiction. Outside the State of South Dakota, he killed someone (and almost another) over a dispute about beer. After being charged for his crimes, Chris took on prison life with no intention of repentance. In full rebellion, he became very active in a prison gang.

This behavior earned Chris solitary confinement, where he was locked up for 23 hours every day. During this time of despair, the Lord did something spectacular in Chris' life. For years, he was identified with a religion that can be quite hostile to Christians. But something caused Chris to request a Bible.

As he began reading God's Word, the truth on the pages started leaping out at him. Before long, Chris found himself in the same situation I had been in at age 19. He didn't have a field or a night sky as background, but in his claustrophobic prison cell, he repented and surrendered to the One who had died so Chris might live.

Chris still has many years to do in prison. Nonetheless, he found the great escape.

After Chris' conversion, prison staff could deal with him much more easily. He began to (and is still learning to) walk in God's Grace and display the fruit of the Spirit (Galatians 5:22-24). His behavior improved to the point it was no longer necessary to keep him on lockdown.

There was only one problem: before his conversion, Chris had gained so many enemies within the prison population, he couldn't be safely released to the general population. As a result, he was sent to South Dakota and Mike Durfee State Prison, where I currently work as pastor of Living Stone Prison Church.

I remember when I first met Chris. He told me his story,

explaining that, because of his former lockdown situation, he'd had minimal contact with chaplains and almost no contact with other believers. He asked about getting baptized.

I told Chris I'd call him to my chapel office to talk about his request. We had just remodeled a 6,000 square foot prison area as a beautiful new house of worship. When Chris entered the new chapel, he was overwhelmed with emotion. He walked across the chapel and into my office, where he sat in a chair and wept for joy.

A few weeks later, I was honored to baptize Chris in the name of the Father, Son, and Holy Spirit.

Chris (a lot like the mare in the intro) had lived a life of extreme confinement, but he decided to take a chance on a life-altering relationship with Jesus. The Savior has now opened to him a life he could never have imagined. He cherishes being a baptized member of the Body of Christ, more than most (if not all) Christians you'll ever meet. I look forward to watching him continue his journey during the rest of his incarceration, walking in the freedom of knowing and being known by Jesus.

When Jesus' hometown (Nazareth) invited Him to speak in the synagogue at the beginning of His ministry launch, He took the scroll with the book of Isaiah and read these words: *"The Spirit of the Lord is upon me, because he has anointed me to proclaim good news to the poor. He has sent me to proclaim liberty to the captives and recovering of sight to the blind, to set at liberty those who are oppressed, to proclaim the year of the Lord's favor* (Luke 4:18-19)."

After he read from the scroll, Jesus declared that *"Today this scripture has been fulfilled in your hearing* (Luke 4:21)." Jesus was saying to His fellow Nazarenes that He was, in fact, the Messiah they had waited for, who would reverse the conditions (poverty, captivity, blindness, oppression) holding them back from living in the Lord's favor.

With His healing power, Jesus delivered people from all sorts of things in the physical realm while He walked the earth. He still does those kinds of things today through the power of the Holy Spirit.

But, I believe the freedom He was talking about has more to do with our spiritual condition.

I realized when I was a teenager that I was morally bankrupt, but Jesus gave me a no-interest loan from His account. I was delivered from my poverty, which is "Good News!"

My friend Chris was imprisoned to his sinfulness and rebellion, and Jesus drew him in and freed him from that captivity. We're told in 2 Corinthians 4:4 that the devil has blinded the minds of unbelievers, so they don't see the glory of Christ. Jesus sheds light on that blindness and has given sight to many who formerly walked in darkness (like Chris and me).

In many ways, I used to feel oppressed by others because I was different. In my youth, I was a rather easy target. Jesus has given me liberty over that oppression. I now realize He can even use my quirkiness for His glory. All these things Jesus has accomplished by offering us His life for ours.

My favorite Greek word is "sozo," which is used in multiple places in the original language of the New Testament. This word is used to describe the work of Jesus and can be defined as "save, heal, or deliver." These things are quite the opposite of the work of Satan, which is to steal, kill, and destroy (John 10:10).

Accepting the sozo life Jesus offers us gives us the escape we need from those things Satan has used to imprison us. The great escape is that Jesus has taken the wrath of God upon Himself so that we captives can be freed. Repentance and surrender are the ingredients that precede a life lived in service to Jesus. "*All have sinned and fallen short of the glory of God*" (Romans 3:23), whether you've murdered or gossiped. All sin must be dealt with equally at the cross. We are all in need of a Savior.

The sentence for sin is death, but thankfully, we can accept Jesus' death on our behalf so we can be redeemed through the gift of Grace through Jesus Christ (Romans 3:24). Accepting Christ's gift of Grace through the cross is not only life-altering, it has eternal implications.

The reality is that, when we leave this earth, we move into a permanent residence with God (heaven) or apart from Him in a place of torment (hell). When I found Jesus (or when He found me), I knew I had a place in eternity with Him. It was that realization which gave me the courage to truly embrace my mortal life here on earth.

If you've already received the gift of God through Grace,

you can marvel at the amazing escape Jesus offers. If you've never cried out to Him, now would be a good time. Just tell God what He already knows: you have lived in darkness and sin. You need Jesus to save you and guide you into a new life.

Giving up your old life and embracing a new one in Christ may be hard, but nothing is more worthwhile.

Reflection Questions
- Why do you think many "crawl through the sewers" of life before embracing true freedom?
- "Fear can hold you prisoner, hope can set you free." What do you think of this statement?
- Contrast the work of Jesus (save, heal, deliver) with the work of Satan (steal, kill, destroy). Do you see those things at work in the world today? If so, describe how they look.
- Look up 2 Corinthians 5:21 in your Bible and ponder the great escape found in the truth that Jesus offers His righteousness (perfection/uprightness) for our sin.

"The size of a challenge should never be measured by what we have to offer. It will never be enough. Furthermore, provision is God's responsibility, not ours. We are merely called to commit what we have—even if it's no more than a sack lunch."

— Charles R. Swindoll

4

ALL THESE THINGS

I remember sitting at a restaurant finishing up my meal when the waiter unexpectedly plopped a dessert in front of me.

Confused, I looked at him.

"It's on the house," he said. "We accidentally made two for another customer."

I had eaten my main meal, but I also got a bonus I didn't even know was coming. It was a foreshadowing of much more that would be "on the house."

After surrendering to Jesus, I joined the church my family attended in Rock Valley, Iowa. I was also compelled to enroll at a local community college and work toward completing my high school diploma, reversing my drop-out status.

I began repairing my relationship with my parents, easing the despair they experienced through my past actions. The critical step was surrendering to the Savior, but I found many bonuses came along with my new lifestyle.

Before I am accused of going full-blown "prosperity gospel" on you, let me explain by using a teaching of Jesus found in Luke 12:22-34.

In these verses, Jesus instructed His followers to be anxious for nothing. He told them God His Father knows that they need things like food and clothes. The Master Teacher explained that God provides for the needs of the birds of the air and the lilies of the field. He assured the people that they were far more valuable than the flowers or the feathered flocks.

He then said this about His follower's tendency to worry: *"Instead, seek his (God's) kingdom, and these things will be added to you (Luke 12:31)."* Jesus said, put first things first, and let God take care of the rest.

I'm telling you this was my experience. I began seeking the Kingdom of God and He started providing for needs in ways I didn't see coming. This is not a "name it and claim it" type of thing. This is God, revealing in the life of one of His children, the needs He wanted to provide for. I have often been surprised by the way in which God provides for my basic needs (food, clothing, etc.). I've been equally shocked by the way in which He gifts us with other things we need for the journey ahead.

One specific need of mine was for someone I could share my life with. Way back in Genesis, God decided it was not good for Adam to be alone (Genesis 2:18). God also decided it was not good for Jason to be alone. For Adam, God created Eve.

For Jason, the search was on.

After my spiritual awakening, I dated a couple of nice girls, but the relationships ended without getting serious. One night, I received a phone call from a girl I hadn't seen for a while. Somehow, I was expecting she would contact me. No person had tipped me off, but God had spoken to me about her on three separate occasions. One of them was the night I threw my cigarettes in the water.

She was one of the girls that stopped and talked to us by the pond that night. Her name was Ruth. She had gotten wind of some of the changes in my life. She was interested in finding out what the new me was like.

I guess Ruth liked Jason 2.0 because, a year and a half later, we became husband and wife. It seemed like I was living in some sort of fairy tale.†

All those years before, as I sat by that pond, God caused me to recognize a need for change if I was to marry the girl of my dreams. But really, it was the relationship with Him I desperately needed. After He added me to His family, He still brought Ruth and me together to fill a need I had for the chapters of life that were to come. She is a woman whose strengths were/are in areas in which I am deficient.

Friends, you can't make up a better story than that! Jesus said, *"Seek the Kingdom first and let God the Father take care of the rest* (Matthew 6:33)." As it pertained to my godly wife and

---

† If I was a musician, I'd write a song titled, "I Was Ruthless Until She Started Chasin' Jason."

many other things that will be covered in future chapters, He did just that.

The subject of seeking the Kingdom first and letting God handle the details from there is an important one in prison. Most men I've witnessed who have come to know Jesus bring a lot of baggage into that relationship. In most cases, baggage dumped onto another person will cause them to crumble. That isn't the case with Jesus. Only He can handle the burdens of our lives and carry us to where we need to go (Matthew 11:28-30).

If I had come into our marriage with the expectation that Ruth was going to fix me and heal all my issues, she would have been crushed by the weight of my burdens. Instead, Jesus dealt with me first, took care of the weight of my sin and gave me a direction for my life, so Ruth and I could begin our journey together with Him in the center.†

I'm always concerned when I suspect either one or both parties planning to marry believe that marriage will heal them. If they don't welcome Jesus into the center of such a union, they'll find themselves at an empty cistern. They're likely to either live in misery much of the time or split up when burdens become too great.

The implications of seeking first the Kingdom is certainly not just about marriage and relationships. It's about all our

---

†   Don't get me wrong, our marriage hasn't been all fuzzy kitty cats and marshmallow Christmas trees. But one of the miracles is, with God, it has been more than we could have ever imagined. (Ephesians. 3:20)

needs. I often have an opportunity to encourage men who find themselves being drawn to Jesus as they deal with broken relationships, addictions, financial stress, pending legal consequences, etc.

My counsel to them is to set all those things aside as much as possible and put first things first. Seek out a relationship with the One who can handle all the baggage in the world.

Once we trust God for eternal salvation, we can also learn to trust Him to direct our lives in a pattern that will work for our good (Romans 8:28). This does NOT mean everything in our lives will be easy or pleasant. It does mean God will be at work in everything to use our circumstances for His glory and for our good.

I look at the disciplines of seeking first the Kingdom and then continuing in an ongoing journey of following Jesus as a challenge for all of us. There's good reason why we're called to live our lives this way. Our problems do not disappear when we come to the cross for the first time (our condemnation does, see Romans 8:1). That's one of the reasons it's foolish to think we can welcome Jesus into our lives and then just go about our business on our own from there. It's like saying I don't want to end up in hell, but I don't want to follow Jesus either.†

We need God's Son for Heaven, and we need Him to take the reins of our lives here on earth. We need Jesus as both Savior and Lord. I'm not suggesting we sit complacently and

---

† This is "fire insurance" Christianity which ignores the consistent call of scripture to repent (turn away) from sin.

just wait for Jesus to fix our problems. On the contrary, we're to take an active role in finding the resolve to walk away from the things that imprison us.

Sometimes people become impatient when fighting things like addiction, just wishing God would instantly heal them. But the truth of the matter is that, when we partner with God to find the power over our addictions and shortcomings, when we put in the work, we are far less likely to walk back into the mess again later. We don't want to go through the process again. We remember well the blood, sweat, and tears it took to escape the mess.

In my experience, addicts who find victory over their vice, whether it be substance abuse, porn, kleptomania or another weakness of the flesh, are individuals who seek first God's Kingdom and then keep their eyes on Jesus as He continues to lead them in victory. Groups such as Celebrate Recovery can be vital to this process as they provide the addict with a community focused on recovery through Jesus Christ.

You may have heard it said we have a God-shaped hole in our lives and, unless we let Him in (seek Him first), we feel the void and try to jam other things into that space. We may even worship other things, either intentionally or simply by letting our thoughts be dominated by them. When Jesus is on the throne of our lives, we keep our idols at bay.

Let me tell you about Dell. He was never sentenced to prison, but years ago Dell was caught up in drug addiction. Drugs threatened to take his life, his family, his possessions.

Things seemed rather hopeless for Dell. But just when it seemed he was at the point of no return, he made "the next right decision"† by checking into rehab. It was there that he took time to reflect on his real problem: an aching void in his life that only God could fill.

I've heard Dell give his testimony at men's retreats and in prisons. During his stint in rehab, he had a powerful encounter in which God pulled Him to a park bench. He was then lifted high in the air by a pair of invisible hands. He was able to look down upon himself sitting on the bench, and over the entire town.

At that moment, surrendering to Jesus, Dell became part of the Kingdom of God, saved by the One who could inhabit the God-shaped hole he'd tried to fill with drugs. That story may be hard for some people to believe. But I do, because I know Dell, and I know his life has never been the same since that experience. He left rehab having put first things first.

Dell and his family have since built a missionary compound in Haiti (Touch of Hope Haiti) that operates an orphanage and a school, builds homes in their community, feeds hungry villagers, and the list goes on and on. To create such a place is a monumental task, especially in a third-world country that lacks much in the way of infrastructure. I've been there multiple times. It's truly a miraculous place.

What an adventure it is when we have our priorities straight.

---

† Remember: it is never too late to make the next right decision.

Dell said, "Yes!" to Jesus and His Kingdom, escaping the prison of addiction and receiving "all these things" he needed for an amazing journey from that point on. God has provided funding, people, time—all that is necessary for the former substance abuser to impact a foreign mission field with the love of Jesus Christ.

I think that is awesome!

God knows we need food. God knows we need clothes and knows exactly what we need to do the tasks He's calling us to do on this earth.

God is for us, not against us. He knows what we need and when we need it. What do you need to get to wherever it is God wants to take you? I don't know, but He does!

The first move is always to accept God's terms of adoption through the cross, to seek His Kingdom first.

Reflection Questions

- Why do you think God asks us to seek His Kingdom before seeking His help with other needs?
- Why do you think it is essential that we recognize Jesus as both Savior and Lord?
- Do you agree that those who partner with God to achieve victory are less likely to go back to their addictions and old ways?
- What problems do you currently have that God could ultimately use for your good and His Glory?

"An unpeaceful mind cannot operate normally. Hence the Apostle teaches us to 'have no anxiety about anything. Deliver all anxious thoughts to God as soon as they arise. Let the peace of God maintain your heart and mind.'" (Philippians 4:6-7)

— *Watchman Nee*

5

THE DANGER OF
PAROLE VIOLATIONS

"So, you must have missed me." This is a comment I often make to returning inmates.

Having a prison congregation is unique in that we are happy to see members of our congregation go, and it's often disappointing to see them return. But, after using the "missed me" line on them, I listen to their stories.

Through listening, I've learned there are many different reasons a man might return to prison. Most often, men of the Living Stone congregation give it to me straight about how they could or should have done things differently.

Parole violations I've heard include: leaving the state without permission; having a dirty drug test; contacting someone they weren't supposed to; failing to keep a job; joining a gang and beating up someone on the order of a leader; etc.

My point in providing this list is that the ways an inmate

can get sent back to prison are numerous. Likewise, numerous things can imprison a person living outside prison walls. Although I experienced many freedoms through surrendering to Christ, in time I found yet another prison.

Married life was challenging for both Ruth and me. We each had plans related to what our marriage should be. Many times, we weren't on the same page, which meant a fair share of arguments.

But we had both been raised to weather the storms of marriage and persevere, which is what we did. We also experienced the joy and newness of carving out a life for ourselves not far from where we both grew up.

Church was a constant in our lives, and we served our congregation in multiple ways. But, of the things that were solid and consistent in our marriage, my work was not one of them.

In my early 20s, I worked for multiple construction companies, managed a horse ranch, did farm work, ran a machine for a manufacturing company, and worked in prison as a corrections officer. The reason I had so many jobs wasn't that I was getting fired.

Honestly, I kept quitting jobs and moving on because I just felt there was something out there that I was MEANT to do instead of just waking up each morning with a job I HAD to do.

The physical part of working I could handle, but the mental part I often found taxing. I struggled to concentrate on completing tasks in the same way I struggled to learn in school. This made aspects of each job mentally painful for me. I found myself once again trying so hard to concentrate and think like a "normal person" does, only to get frustrated and feel like a failure all over again.

In those days, in our area, a young man with a decent work ethic could find a job rather quickly. So, for a few years, due to my restless mind, I changed my work like I changed my socks.

There were other stressors present as well for a young married man. Not only did I have to adjust to being married, but we began a family, adding three kids to the mix. We had to learn how to be parents as well.

None of these things are unusual, but these normal stresses of life began to add up to a load I felt I couldn't bear. My self-worth was in a much better place than it was when I was a child. Still, I walked around with the idea that I would fail most of the time in areas "ordinary people" could handle with relative ease, like fatherhood or advancing in a career.

I had a painful uneasiness of mind I didn't understand. That's when my addictive side started coming out again. In the self-help book for ADHD adults, *You Mean I'm Not Lazy, Stupid or Crazy?!*, the author says this about addiction: "At its core, addiction to anything is about feeling not good enough and trying desperately to grasp at something outside yourself for a 'feel good' fix."

My primary "fix" those days was to play hard after work in hopes I could find peace through enjoyable hobbies. For a time, I became somewhat addicted to horse training. This is a great hobby I hope to enjoy again later in life. At the time, I poured so much time and energy into learning new techniques about training horses to ride, that I neglected my young family.

I still enjoy fishing, but back then, I became addicted to the pursuit of trophy bass. Obsessed, I often headed to a lake immediately after work. Looking back, I realize I was always on the go, mostly because I feared what my mind would do if I stopped.

But the fact is that humans must rest. We simply must stop at some point. And it was in the evenings that my mind started to run wild with negativity. I had tried to outrun fear, but it caught up with me in my late 20s.

I began having anxiety attacks. Depression followed right behind. These were new conditions for me. The despair I thought I'd left in the rear view mirror moved in for another round, feeding off my underlying belief that somehow, some way, I would always eventually fail.

My favorite definition of the type of fear I experienced in those days is an acronym: False Evidence Appearing Real (F.E.A.R.). I began worrying about everything. What people would think of my old work truck, tragedies that might befall my kids, things I might do to let my customers down (I was for the most part self-employed doing construction at that time).

I tried many different medications but found no long-term solution. My negative thoughts were ruling my life. I remember sitting up at night, unable to sleep, just thinking to myself that I might have to live out the rest of my life, barely even wanting to survive. I had escaped a former prison of low self-worth, but now it appeared as if I had violated parole and was heading back into another personal prison. It was a clear-cut case of "false evidence appearing real."

Through it all, I tried my best to conceal my issues. I spoke to a couple people about it. One friend suggested I pray about it. I almost smacked him. Prayer. Of course! I never thought of that (savor the sarcasm)!

I was, in fact, praying all along. For a time, it didn't seem my prayers were reaching the heavenly realm. Now I know God was at work in it all, (Romans 8:28) and breakthroughs were on the way.

One day I was listening to a baseball game on the radio† and heard an ad about an anxiety and depression program you could order through the mail. I called about it and learned it wasn't cheap. But I was desperate to climb out of my situation. I ordered it.

The program was called, *Attacking Anxiety and Depression.* As I dove into it, I learned I had a polluted mind full of false evidence I had accepted as real. My real problem wasn't that I was somehow doomed to fail. My thought life was a cognitive landfill of waste that needed to be recycled or permanently disposed of.

I began practicing a process I learned through the program (which I continue to this day) of monitoring my thoughts and

† Baseball isn't always the best choice when you're already anxious and depressed.

swapping negative lies for truth. I literally started thinking about how I was thinking all day long.

I really believe much of the anxiety and depression people suffer from could be cured by changing our thought patterns. I still have bouts of anxiety and depression (mostly seasonal), but I'm healed in the fact that these things no longer dictate how I live. They don't hold me back from doing anything.

It's important to note that this program's concept regarding my thoughts is quite scriptural, especially when I recognized that the attacks on my mental well-being were very much spiritual in nature.

2 Corinthians 10:4–5 says: "*For the weapons of our warfare are not of the flesh but have divine power to destroy strongholds. We destroy arguments, and every lofty opinion raised against the knowledge of God, and take every thought captive to obey Christ.*"

I like the way Levi Lusko put it in his book (which I recommend for the anxious and/or depressed) titled, "*I Declare War.*" Lusko said, "I don't believe in positive thinking as a replacement for God but as a response to God."

God used the tools in the attacking anxiety program to bring me out of my prison of despair and help me respond appropriately to His goodness. He also began reviving my desire to wholeheartedly live for Him.

Over the years since I surrendered, I bore fruit (signs of belief-John 15:4-5), but I was sort of a two-apple tree. Spiritually speaking, truth be told, I had no idea how to blossom and pollinate to bear more fruit. My life seemed stuck. But, as my state of well-being began bouncing back, welling up inside me was a new-found inclination to serve God in a greater capacity. I remember standing in front of my shop one day, thinking about how I'd like to get serious about my faith. Along with that thought, I had to admit I didn't know how to even start. God had an answer to that as you'll see in the next chapter.

I'd hate to go back to those years when my emotional well-being was so damaged. But I must recognize that God used that season of my life to prepare me for the season I'm currently in. Many men that come into the prison system suffer from anxiety and depression. Some have been under that influence their entire life.

Take James, for instance. He grew up with the pangs of never knowing his father, who was incarcerated. James longed to be loved and accepted, but negative voices flooded his mind and distracted him from the Good Shepherd's (Jesus') voice, the One who longed to claim James as one of His flock.

James started a family hoping that having his own kids would somehow fill the void inside. But brokenness and pain persisted. He drank to soften the blow. One night things got out of control. In a drunken stupor he became violent, committing atrocities he has regretted every day since. Those acts sent him to prison.

I met James shortly after he was incarcerated. At that time, he was at a point of humility, his heart was softened.

With a mind clear of alcohol, James was able to hear and respond to the voice of the Savior, much to the delight of his praying mother.

James' incarceration was relatively short (a little over three years), but during his time in prison, I witnessed him grow in faith and in the knowledge of the Word. He was even voted by our congregation to be on Living Stone's Leadership Board.

But it wasn't always smooth sailing. James still battled the type of negative inner voices that do not originate with the Good Shepherd.

One day James found himself at a crossroads. He received bad news on both the family and legal fronts. He was starting to slide back into old habits, thinking he'd been abandoned by God. I got wind of his struggles and called him into my prison office.

I could see it on his face as James sat down. When he opened his mouth, what I heard sounded eerily familiar to voices I'd listened to a little over a decade before. He felt rejected by other Christians. It seemed he didn't matter much to God anymore. He felt perhaps his transformation was a sham.

James was being lied to. On that day, he was believing the "father of lies" and buying into false evidence that appeared real (F.E.A.R.). I didn't get angry with him. Instead, I was quick to point out the spiritual warfare at work in his current pattern of thinking. I remember tearing up as I told him I had every intention of walking with him to get to the other side of the battle he was in.

I'm pleased to report that James bounced back from his little bout of "stinking thinking." In fact, he grew even stronger in his faith in the months that followed. Shortly before he was released on parole, James got more bad news. I kept my eye on him to see how he'd respond. This time he seemed rather unfazed. When I asked him about it, he said he'd learned now that God can get him through the tough times. James is currently out of the physical prison, and praise God he's learned to escape the prison of toxic thinking as well.

Friends, that's what Jesus was talking about when He told His followers in John 16:33: *"In the world you will have tribulation. But take heart; I have overcome the world."* Again, in Matthew 7:24-25, He says that those who build their house (life) on His words will be able to stand in the storms of life.

Jesus' sheep still experience life's problems, but the Good Shepherd never leaves us unattended during those times. I had a hard time believing that while I went through my struggles with anxiety and depression. Now, looking back, I see it clearly.

Reflection Questions

- Why is it important to recognize the devil as the "father of lies?"

- Do you find it easy or difficult to take every thought captive to Christ? Are you willing to examine your thoughts for one day to see what's rolling around up there?

- Why do you think some Christians are reluctant to admit they have a problem with things like depression and anxiety? How might the church respond to these issues?

- Why do you think a life built on the words of Jesus can weather a storm?

*"Either sin is with you, lying on your shoulders,
or it is lying on Christ, the Lamb of God.
Now if it is lying on your back, you are lost;
but if it is resting on Christ, you are free,
and you will be saved."*

— Martin Luther

6

No, Really,
You Are Free!

Although it no longer has an unhealthy grip on my life, I still very much enjoy casting for bass.†

Most of the time, I practice the catch and release method of fishing, just doing it for the thrill and not the meat. Sometimes I ponder making a meal out of the fish I catch, so I throw them into the live well. If I decide to release them later, I often notice a rather interesting phenomenon which can happen when fish suddenly find themselves free.

Sometimes those I return to the lake swim in place as if still in the live well. I want to scream, *"SWIM! SWIM! SWIM!"* But I'd be too worried that others on the lake might question my sanity.

Truth is, after an extended time in captivity, fish can

---

† Casting is the ADHD approved method of fishing.

temporarily forget how to behave once freedom is restored. At times I've had to slap the water to jolt them awake so they can swim off into the sunset.

As a pastor, it can be even more challenging to convince God's people they can live in Christ's freedom. Galatians 5:1 makes this claim: *"For freedom Christ has set us free; stand firm therefore, and do not submit again to a yoke of slavery."*

In context, this verse talks specifically about the law God gave to Moses and freedom from Old Testament practices such as circumcision. The cross of Jesus Christ has freed us from being bound to the law of Moses. The cross of Jesus Christ has also freed us from the bondage of sin. Galatians 5:1 invites the Christ follower to embrace that freedom and not submit ourselves to the *"yoke"* of slavery anymore.

If I were a fish, there would be no way I'd jump back into the live well upon my release. But as I mentioned earlier, sometimes there's a moment of limbo as if the gilled creature questions whether it's truly free.

I lived in that same limbo for much of my life. I'd heard about this freedom we had in Jesus Christ, freedom from sin (not freedom to sin, see Romans 6:1-2), freedom from following the strict religious code of the law. But something inside me questioned that freedom. I lived my life much like the fish that swims in place, afraid freedom in Christ is too good to be true.

In my early 30s, I found myself freed from the debilitating conditions of anxiety disorder and depression that had plagued me in previous years. As I mentioned earlier, out of thankfulness to God for answered prayer, I found myself wanting to serve Him. But I didn't know the where or the how and, honestly, the idea of it frightened me. As far as I'd come in my walk with Christ, the underlying fear of failure that dogged me my entire life held me back from fully embracing the possibilities.

One element of the anxiety and depression program I completed included a challenge to do something I had formerly held back from doing out of fear (or more accurately, F.E.A.R.). After pondering for a bit how to step out of my comfort zone, I thought of a Christian retreat invitation Ruth and I received. It would be held at Inspiration Hills, a nearby church camp. We decided to try it.

This was a massive stretch for me as I still struggled to trust people in social settings. I went to the men's portion of the retreat, committed to facing the fear of not exactly knowing what I was getting into while hanging out with a bunch of strangers for a weekend.

As the weekend proceeded, I realized beyond a shadow of a doubt I had been set up by God to be there. Throughout that weekend, the message of God's Grace through Jesus Christ was presented so powerfully. This really wasn't anything new to me. I'd accepted that Grace when I surrendered to Christ at age 19.

But I needed to hear just how profound and freedom producing God's Grace could be in someone's life. During the retreat there were many speakers, some of them pastors gifted in bringing out scriptural truth. Others were farmers, welders, construction guys, and other average Joes who spoke and guided us through each day.

As I heard testimonies of how God had transformed people's lives and was using them to do amazing things in our generation, something started coming alive inside me. I needed to hear that. Sometimes in our churches, we talk about the God of the Bible and the amazing things He did, without also recognizing that the same God is at work through the power of the Holy Spirit today. He's using pastors, blue-collar folks and businessmen alike to do His work of pointing others towards the cross in the 21st century!

I began realizing I was a fish who'd already been caught up by God's grace. But I hadn't been swimming. I'd been treading water, but that was all about to change as I was drenched in the truth and with a power that was hitting me square in the heart.

During that weekend in February 2007, three crucial things happened. First, I rededicated my life to Jesus and asked Him to take full control. Second, I found multiple Christ-centered friendships with like-minded people who wanted to live out a faith that wasn't just one part of their life. It was the driving force at the center of their life. These friendships are still in place to this very day.

I think of my friend, Bruce, who also dedicated his life to serving God at the retreat. God gave him a specific calling as a prayer warrior that weekend. I'm so thankful to God for the way this man and others have since prayed me through the many different seasons of life I encountered, with all their joys and challenges.

The third thing that happened to me was something I could never have imagined. It was the answer to so many questions I had about how to serve God in greater capacities than before.

Late one night, during the retreat, I found myself unable to sleep. Wide awake, I sat at a booth in the gaming area of the retreat center, reading a book on sharing one's faith. Suddenly, I was struck with a feeling that was somewhat familiar, yet different than I'd ever experienced. This moving and powerful presence came over me. I heard God speak to my heart, calling me into a life of serving Him.

Before that moment, I had heard of the Baptism of the Holy Spirit, but I never thought such a thing would happen to me. As I recognized what was happening, I tried to argue saying, "Me? Me?" If it hadn't been for the overwhelming power of the Spirit, I'm sure I would have come up with some great reasons why He couldn't call me.

"But God, remember my .90 GPA that one semester in high school? God, you must have forgotten how I threw my book in the trash and stomped out of Mr. Feenstra's Bible class junior year of high school! Oh, I know! How about the time I raided the senior's locker room when they were in PE and was able to come out with a bunch of cash, and someone else got all the blame?† Surely all those things disqualify me from what you want me to do."

But, here's the deal. Because God drew me to that retreat, I had now come to the point where I realized beyond any shadow of a doubt that the Son of God, the most powerful person in the universe, came down and died so I may be free. Not kind of free, not mostly free. Completely free in God's Grace. Therefore, I have been given a clean slate. My excuses held no power over God's new call on my life.

As I write this, it's been some 12 years since these life-changing events took place. Some thought it would be a phase that would pass. But I tell you the truth when I say that from that day forward a courage was upon me to declare the Gospel message of Jesus Christ as I'd always wanted to. What I needed all along was a filling of the Spirit.

Friends, I've met many people in my day who believe their checkered past disqualifies them from serving the Lord or they don't think they have the necessary abilities. I completely understand those thoughts because they held me back for a long time.

This is where I love the verses from which Living Stone Church pulls its name. 1 Peter 2:4–5 says: "*As you come to Him, a Living Stone rejected by men but in the sight of God chosen and precious, you yourselves like living stones are being built up as a spiritual house, to be a holy priesthood, to offer spiritual*

---

† Don't worry Rob. I won't tell anyone that you were my partner in crime that day.

sacrifices acceptable to God through Jesus Christ."

You see, through Jesus, the Living Stone, God accepts our "spiritual sacrifices," those ways in which we serve Him out of our thankfulness. In other words, Grace makes our imperfect attempts at serving God something pleasing to Him. And the Holy Spirit, who came upon the disciples at Pentecost, still comes upon believers today to equip them for their own unique calling.

As I would find out, God doesn't call the qualified. He qualifies the called by the power of the cross and the indwelling of the Holy Spirit.

Our work has primarily been in the prison systems of South Dakota, but we've been in some other corrections facilities as well. For those in prison ministry today, you are probably aware of the Angola prison in Louisiana. In January of 2017, Ruth and I traveled to Angola with a couple friends to experience firsthand what God has done there.

You see, Angola is famous for having been a horribly bloody place that made a big turnaround under the direction of Warden Burl Cain. My copy of Warden Cain's book about Angola's transformation, *Cain's Redemption,* is signed by Burl, "To my friend Jason." I don't know Warden Cain as well as I'd like to. But after we visited Louisiana, he came to South Dakota and spoke at Living Stone's annual banquet. He also met with a group of state politicians who wanted to hear about his ground-breaking work in prison reform. His life story is very inspiring.

One big thing Warden Cain brought into the prison (in addition to some beautiful chapel buildings) is a seminary program within the walls of Angola through which inmates can complete a biblical degree in partnership with the New Orleans Baptist Seminary. Burl's theory is that biblical instruction gives birth to morality, and moral people do not rape, murder, steal, etc. Once men graduate from this seminary, they are given jobs to do within the prison, including caring for the spiritual needs of the sick, leading Bible studies on their units, and preaching in the chapels. These tasks are carried out by trained inmates who have authentically surrendered their lives to Jesus Christ. Over time they have transformed the prison.

Multiple inmates who have completed the program and been released have gone on to pastor churches on the outside as well. It wasn't personal qualification that caused these men to succeed. God called them, and the Holy Spirit has equipped them.

The men in this program have not let their past dictate how they can be used in the future. One man, whose story is told in chapter seven of Cain's book, goes by the name Eugene "Bishop" Tanniehill. If ever there was a man who was unqualified to lead because of past mistakes, it would be him.

As a young man, Eugene killed a local pastor. In his own words, he said: "I slew a man of God. I was a heathen, and I destroyed a man of God." Sentenced to life plus 25 years for the crime, he ended up in Angola. There he contemplated ending his life until he cried out to God in repentance in 1963.

He said of that night: "I don't think a person can ever forget the transforming power of God's grace." The Bishop earned that title because, starting that same night, he began declaring the message of repentance and surrender to Jesus to fellow inmates. He was spit on, had human waste thrown on him, but couldn't keep his mouth shut about the freedom he found in Christ. He shined a light in the country's darkest place and witnessed firsthand the power of God sweep over Angola and transform it.

In 2007, after 50 years of incarceration, then Governor of Louisiana, Kathleen Blanco, released the Bishop to do the Lord's work on the outside. Unable to ignore the Spirit's promptings to continue to declare the Gospel to inmates, Tanniehill found himself accepting many invitations to go into various prisons with the message of hope and freedom found in Jesus Christ.

A person under the influence of God's grace can find themselves free regardless of outside circumstances. Once a person really understands the power of God's amazing Grace, coupled with the power and guidance of the Holy Spirit, things that seemed formerly impossible suddenly are within reach.

Reflection Questions

- Why do you think so many people misunderstand freedom in Christ? Are you *"swimming in place"* at times? Why or why not?

- What fear might be holding you back from doing something God could use to your benefit and His glory? I challenge you to pray about going through with it. *"God doesn't call the qualified, He qualifies the called."* What do you think of this statement?

- Do you find it challenging to believe you can serve the Lord? If so, what steps could you take starting today to allow the Holy Spirit to build up your courage? (See Luke 11:13)

"The grace of God doesn't simply invite us to follow . . . it teaches us to follow."

— *Kyle Idleman*

7

STEPS IN
FREEDOM

Of all the Biblical characters of the Old and New Testaments, I identify most with Peter. I understand Peter's feelings of unworthiness when, for the first time, he met Jesus, and the Savior performed the miraculous catch of fish. *"But when Simon Peter saw it, he fell down at Jesus' knees, saying, 'Depart from me, for I am a sinful man, O Lord* (Luke 5:8).'"

In the presence of such an amazing man, Peter felt shameful, as if he shouldn't be in the same geographic location as Jesus. I don't know about you, but I've been there. Like Peter, I've learned that Jesus accepts me despite what I think of myself.

Of the many other episodes in Peter's life, where I could have been his understudy and jumped right into the scene, the one that comes to mind is the story of the Mount of

Transfiguration (Mark 9:2-13). In this narrative, Jesus takes Peter, James, and John up on a high mountain. There Jesus is transfigured. His divine attributes shine through as he appears intensely white. Not only that, but Elijah and Moses, straight out of the Old Testament, join the party. This was a real mountaintop experience!

Peter is taking it all in, and we read this from verse 5: *"And Peter said to Jesus, 'Rabbi, it is good that we are here. Let us make three tents, one for you and one for Moses and one for Elijah.'"*

You see, I'm like Peter in that, when I have a mountaintop experience with Jesus, I'd love to set up camp and just live in that feeling the rest of my life. But the mountaintops are there to prepare us for the plains or even, at times, valleys we must serve in and through.

One of my mountain top events occurred during the retreat where I was drenched in truth, filled with the Holy Spirit, called into ministry and experienced Jesus in a way I never imagined possible . . . now what? I would have loved to set up a couple tents and just stay with Jesus a while longer. But, like Peter, I had to come down from the mountain and prepare to serve my Savior in other terrains of life.

Following that experience, there were so many questions for which I had no immediate answers. I was uncertain about what the next years of my family's life would look like. Still, somehow, I knew all I had to do in the present moment was be faithful in little things.

I joined a Bible study and started another one with a group

of friends. Devotions and worship, which had been a compartmentalized part of my life, became my life's fuel.

Out of the overflow of my heart, and not from duty or guilt, I began volunteering in our church and community. It was clear that what the Lord had started in me was something He planned to continue. I was focused, but the future seemed overwhelming.

I recall the words of a former inmate who was about to leave the prison. "Pastor Jason," he said, "I don't know if I'll be following Jesus a year from now." God's grace had grabbed this man while he was in prison. Now I was confused by his comment. I said nothing, just gave him a puzzled look.

He continued, "I don't know if I'll be following Jesus in a year, but I'll be following Him tomorrow, and then tomorrow I'm going to commit to following Him the next day and then that day I'll commit to Him the following day." The great thing about it is that if he followed that formula (to my knowledge he did) for 365 days, he followed Jesus for a year. The results are the same. He was just telling me he could only do it one day, one step at a time. I appreciated his approach because it goes well with Jesus' teachings about not getting wrapped up in tomorrow's worries (Matthew 6:34).

His words reminded me that this same approach works in my own life. One day, one step at a time so as not to be overwhelmed. By keeping my focus on Jesus through daily obedience, I was striving to persevere and keep my sights on the calling I knew was on my life.

But, what did it all mean? Would my fears and doubts eventually hold me back from following through with whatever was next? Would Ruth be on board with the changes I felt were coming?

Martin Luther King Jr. once said, "Faith is taking the first step, even when you don't see the whole staircase." Had Ruth and I seen the whole "staircase," there were many things about this adventure that could have caused us to be like Jonah (Jonah 1:3) and run from God's call. But one step at a time God began revealing His will and the path we were to take.

God answered my question about Ruth's involvement in a very timely manner. She attended a women's retreat shortly after I attended mine. The Lord blew her away with His goodness as well. During that retreat, God gave her a vision of something which provided us with the necessary confidence to move forward into what seemed impossible. She saw me clearly in a seminary classroom pursuing a pastoral degree. You see, I had been trying to conjure up alternative options for launching into ministry WITHOUT schooling.

I was in no way trying to argue with God. However, the thought of sitting in a stuffy classroom full of holier-than-thou seminary types in deep discussions on whether or not Adam had a belly button held no appeal.† Of course, I had no idea what seminary was like. Two months before this, I would have laughed at anyone who suggested that I go, recommend-

---

†   Adam was never in a womb, no belly button-case closed!!!

ing they seek out mental treatment. How could someone who so despised classrooms and textbooks possibly pursue a Master's degree?

However, Ruth, being sure of what God had revealed to her, arranged a visit with Sioux Falls Seminary. We had known multiple pastors who had studied there. During our first visit at the seminary, the staff was very welcoming, wanting to help us discern God's call on our lives. No one made us feel like we didn't belong. Despite many lingering questions, God's voice whispered through it all, "Just take the next step. I've got this."

That first year after my call, even though it still seemed a crazy idea to pursue education, I decided to get my feet wet and take a couple courses at a local college. I took a computer course (I was computer illiterate) and a speech class (which terrified me). Those two subjects seemed challenging yet beneficial for meeting whatever tasks the future might bring.

I was shocked when I got through the semester and received A's in these courses. I hadn't had grades like that since—well—I never had grades like that, period. God was revealing that His plan for our lives would happen in His time, in His way. We didn't need to see the whole staircase.

We've been taking this pleasant stroll through the story God has written in my life. However, each of us who strives to live out God's purpose has their own story. I never tire of hearing stories of how Jesus can redeem broken lives.

Gary was one of the first men I became acquainted with while ministering at Mike Durfee State Prison. When working as an educator, Gary reacted unlawfully to a stressful life situation. His poor decisions led him to "catching" a felony.†

Many inmates have a prison "look," but Gary appears to be someone from the suburbs you'd see grilling with his family on a Sunday afternoon.

That being said, Gary was serving eight years in prison and would have to figure out for himself how to live behind the fence. Prison life, like most things, is something a person discerns day by day and step by step.

When a new inmate (a "fish" in prison lingo) comes into the prison and asks to visit me, there's a speech they're likely to hear. I tell them the amount of time the judge gave them is out of their hands, where they are housed in the prison system is out of their hands, and the schedule they'll be asked to keep is out of their hands.

The thing they can control is how they use their time. I also add that how inmates use their time dictates whether or not incarceration was a wasted season, or if God is glorified as they allow Him to alter the course of their lives.

Since Gary was there before I came, I didn't give him the spiel. But he played a role in the inspiration for that speech. You see, when Gary plugged into the Christian community at MDSP, he was encouraged by one of the musicians there to try his hand at learning to play an instrument. Gary had no musical background whatsoever, but step-by-step he learned

---

† Most guys wish they could treat their felony like a bass, catch and release.

to play the keyboard and sing.

Because of his incarceration, Gary was able to find and foster musical gifts he never knew he had. He added songwriting to his resume and has successfully produced a CD of original songs, all of which glorify God. He's been out of prison for a couple years now and continues to write songs. He's participated in multiple praise bands in churches he has attended on the "outs."

Gary gave his incarceration to Jesus and used it for the Savior's glory. Therefore, it was not wasted. It has produced lasting spiritual fruit.

Gary is a rather inspiring example of what can happen in a surrendered life, but not all of us have musical gifts. Thankfully not everyone has to go to prison to find their God-glorifying gifts. I'm reminded of those weight loss ads where they tell you about their *"amazing"* product. They say something like, "Bubba lost 167 pounds in 7 weeks using our revolutionary fat-burning eucalyptus leaf tonic!!!!" This might put us on the edge of our seats, but then the disclaimer comes at the end. "Results may vary." In that case, results will vary because the claims are trumped up and aimed at our credit cards.

But as it pertains to following Jesus, results will vary as well. Peter followed Jesus step by step, day by day and was a foundational figure in the very first Church. Gary followed Jesus step by step, day by day and has sung the praises of the Savior for all to hear. I followed Jesus step by step, day by day. Over the past decade, He has written my story in a way

I could have never imagined since I contemplated whether I was really supposed to go to seminary.

However, the call of Jesus in your life will likely mean something completely different. I like to say that, "You don't have to do what I do (and probably shouldn't), but do something (to lift up the name of Jesus)." I know that if God willed that I remain a carpenter, He would have given me ample opportunity to serve Him with those gifts, as I've seen others do. I hope and pray that you sincerely evaluate your life. If you recognize a lack of *"fruit"* (God-glorifying results), I hope you begin the process of praying about what God would have you do and be prepared to step daily into the path He will unfold before you.

Reflection Questions

- What do you think of this statement? "Mountaintops (powerful encounters with God) are there to prepare us for the plains and even at times valleys we are to serve in and through."

- Martin Luther King Jr. once said, "Faith is taking the first step, even when you don't see the whole staircase." Why do you think God most often gives us just one step at a time instead of showing us the whole staircase?

- What do you think about Gary's story? What does his story reveal about God's character?

- What fruit-bearing things has God asked you to do? In what ways do you think He is asking you to serve Him in the future?

"God will ensure my success in accordance with His plan, not mine."

— Francis Chan

8

ALL THINGS POSSIBLE

I've heard it said that context is the breakfast of champions (sorry Wheaties). Context is the set of circumstances surrounding an event which helps us better understand the words and actions of said event.

In today's world, where a person can be recorded at any time and in any place, context proves to be very important. For instance, someone could take a video of me smacking my Aunt Cheryl in the back of the head while we are watching a 4th of July parade. This video could go viral, and my ministry accreditations may be stripped from me as I appear to be violent and out of control.

But, let's say, for example, that what the camera didn't catch was a giant wasp landing on my aunt's hair, preparing to inject its venom under her skin and into her skull. Adding this context to the story clears my reputable name and allows me to continue in my work. Context is essential!

Matthew 19:26 is one scripture verse that's often taken out of context. It's part of a conversation Jesus is having with His disciples, saying this: "With man this is impossible, but with God all things are possible." If we "cherry-pick" this verse out of context and apply it to our lives, it could lead us to believe that we are not limited in any way because we are people of God and with Him, it's all possible.

But, in context, Jesus' words were a follow-up to explaining that it's easier for a camel to go through the eye of a needle than for a rich man to enter the Kingdom of God. This was in reference to the rich young man who refused to give up his wealth to follow Jesus. This young man's problem wasn't so much that he had money, it's that his money had him.

What Jesus was saying is that God can make it miraculously possible for those who are wealthy to deny the temptation to love their money and have a heart for Jesus, which guarantees them a place in God's Kingdom. Simply put, God can and does remove obstacles of the heart that otherwise would trick affluent people into trusting in their wealth and forfeiting the Grace that could be theirs.

In my journeys, I've come across many wealthy folks who are generous with their money, seeing it as a gift from God that they are called to share. These are the type of people I believe would give up their wealth if holding on to it meant they wouldn't be able to follow Jesus. In many instances, God allows them to be caretakers of their money, giving them the ability to bless others.

They're the ones who keep many of the God-glorifying ministries funded to do valuable work for God's Kingdom.

God makes possible things He wants that would otherwise be impossible. This includes prompting rich believers to put their trust in Him and not in their money. This does not happen apart from the guidance of the Holy Spirit.

Very similar to Matthew 19:26 are the words of Philippians 4:13. *"I can do all things through him who strengthens me."* These words are sometimes used as a motto for an underdog softball team striving to win their league or a teenage boy who takes on the blazing wing challenge at Buffalo Wild Wings.

But, if we pull in some context from verses 11-12, we see that the famous Philippians 4:13 is about God giving the Apostle Paul everything he needs (at times through the generosity of God's people) to do the Lord's work in proclaiming the Good News about Jesus in both good times and difficult seasons. Once again, this is something God wants in Paul's life that isn't possible apart from the work of the Holy Spirit.

I do hope God blesses your ragtag softball team or your decision to gobble down 12 spicy little chicken legs within six minutes. But that's not what the verse is about. The point could be made in situations like these by saying, "If your softball team wins by 10 runs or loses by 10 runs and your resolve to follow Jesus is the same, you're getting at the heart of this verse."

God can and does empower us to do things that are not possible on a human level. But, we cannot and should not expect Him to do miraculous things in our lives that bear no fruit for the Kingdom or are apart from His will for us. As we mature in faith, our prayers begin to line up with what God wants to do.

I was very aware that responding to God's call on my life was impossible on my own (like a rich man entering heaven). I would need to lean on Him every step of the way, through good days and bad. Eventually, I was accepted into Sioux Falls Seminary as a full-time student seeking a Master's in Divinity Degree† to become a pastor.

In my early seminary days, I remember looking at other students and listening to their questions and comments in class. "So, this is what God's called people are like," I'd think, excluding myself from that group. I still carried that stinking thinking that said, "Even though I am far more in God's eyes than I ever thought, I am somehow still 'less than' the others in my same situation." These thoughts were some of the garbage the Lord was still working out of me.

There were highs and lows during these years, but I was able to keep my focus on the Savior, in whose will all things are possible.

The whole idea of seminary was miraculously and crazily impossible to me. I was faithful to take this step in the journey, but I knew if I tried it in my own power, with my distracted mind, facing classes like Greek and Hebrew would not result

† I really don't think a person can master the divine. Instead, we should let the Divine master us.

in anything more than despair. What I learned, however, is that God had a solution for what seemed like an insurmountable problem. You see, this was the point in my life where I discovered I could indeed learn at a high level. I just had to approach learning from a different angle than most.

On that note, my mind flashes back to a rare episode of triumph coming out of my second-grade year. Math was a giant struggle for me, and I remember working through multiplication tables with much mental anguish. But something clicked when we got to the last single-digit number.

As I looked at the multiplication table, I recognized a pattern related to the number 9. All I had to do was take the number I wanted to multiply times 9, let's say it's 3, take it times 10 instead and then go back the amount of the original number. So, 3 times 10 equals 30 minus 3 equals 27. The correct answer to 3 times 9 is 27, and it worked for every figure.

You may not understand the logic behind that thinking (you weird conventional thinker), but my point is that I nailed that quiz and had it done before anyone else. To have simply taken 3 times 9 to get 27 would have been hard for me then, but I found another way that made sense to my mind. (This is also why some people have difficulty working with me—my brain works differently.)

Had there been a camera in that classroom, I'm quite sure my second-grade teacher would have reviewed the film to find out how I cheated. In seminary, God taught me that my strange mind could come up with alternative ways to remember Greek and Hebrew words. My unorthodox way of thinking was even appreciated by both my theology and biblical professors as I made connections to the truth of God's word in ways they'd probably never seen before.

During my seminary years, I had to learn how to type after formerly swearing I'd never touch a computer in my life.† I also had to concede that the Lord was asking me to preach His Word from the pulpit. I was absolutely terrified to speak publicly.

I recall the first time I was asked to give my testimony in church on a Sunday afternoon. Ruth encouraged me to say yes to the opportunity, and for weeks ahead of time, I lay awake at night, sometimes plotting revenge against her. I remember walking towards the church building with my anxiety level ramped up to about 13 on a scale of 1-10. But as I crossed the threshold and entered the sanctuary, a peace washed over me, and I got to the point I was eager to grab the microphone.

After sharing what God was doing in my life, I sat down. A friend from our church family sat near me. With tears in her eyes, she said, "That was the Holy Spirit!" She was correct. To this day, I ask the same Spirit that gave me peace and clarity to do so every time I speak. The same God that can direct a rich man into the Kingdom of Heaven can lead me to speak on His behalf. If it is God's will, all things are possible!

And God had answers for more than just the seminary classes and the fear of speaking. This cliché you may have

---

† It's better to swear to never use a computer than to swear at one . . . unfortunately I've done both.

heard rings true: "If God brings you to it, He'll bring you through it."

Seminary costs money, of course, but the most significant expense for us was my need to focus on school and work sparingly. Ruth was just getting started as a real estate agent. We wondered how we'd pay bills for our family of five. But in faith, we proceeded anyway.

Ruth went on a real-estate selling spree during those years. It completely covered my lack of wages. We didn't know that would happen. It wasn't in our plans whatsoever. But God did it because He wanted to take care of us and remind us that this whole thing was His idea.

I recall a time a few years ago when an inmate named Sam came to me with an impossible idea. He suggested that the Living Stone Prison Church put on a full-day event in which we offered a meal to the entire prison population in conjunction with a program in which the Gospel message was presented.

Let me be clear that, in the time that we've been working in the Mike Durfee State Prison, the Warden(s) and their staff have been supportive of what we do. However, safety and security must take priority over any special event. I expected the proposed idea would be a bust. However, with my mustard seed of faith, I put together a project application for the occasion with little hope that it would happen.

I was amazed when the top prison staff reviewed the proposal and decided they could handle security for the event. That first year, in August, we had a picnic dinner, our

"Freedom Feed," which included burgers donated by a local farmer. The men were fed physically and spiritually, and I got a chance to speak and proclaim the Gospel to multitudes of inmates that had never come to church. Following the event, some of them began to regularly attend Living Stone.

Every year since, we've been able to hold the "Freedom Feed" in August. My wife's organizational skills aid in working out details for these mega-gatherings. Almost every inmate in the place comes whether they're friendly towards the Christian faith or not. Prison staff does a great job of supervising and establishing safe and secure ways to pull it off.

These one-day events always bear Kingdom fruit. They might come for the potato chips and a burger, but they often leave having been touched by God's power and Grace, some for the very first time. The last couple of years, we've partnered with Lifelight based in Sioux Falls, South Dakota. This group brings in speakers and musicians and has even brought in a Christian Motocross group, Zerogravity, that flips motorcycles in the air and shares the Gospel with the inmates.

After the 2018 event, one man wrote me a note, saying, "It was as if the prison disappeared during the Freedom Feed, and I heard the Lord speaking clearly to me." God wanted that man to have that experience. He wanted the Freedom Feed to happen, and it did. All things are possible with Him.

My apologies to Sam for thinking he was crazy, but all praise and Glory to God for surprising me with His goodness.

The journey Ruth and I have been on has been full of surprises. I entered seminary planning on battling to get grades good enough to simply pass. Instead, when it was all said and done, my GPA was in the 3.5 range. All things are possible with God.

He also gave me a completely unexpected gift at the end of my seminary days. In my last year of theological education, I learned there was a banquet before graduation. I had no idea what the event was about, I just knew we had to dress nice, there would be food, and I was supposed to be there. At one point in the evening, it came time for awards to be presented. Partially distracted, (if ADHD is a superpower, a squirrel is the kryptonite), I was stunned to hear my name announced to receive a Bible for the "Church Ministry Award." This honor goes to a graduating seminary student that has displayed excellence in pastoral ministry.

I remember my confusion as the speaker announced the award. She said, "For 2011 this award is presented to Jason (there's another Jason in our class?) Heath (Oh wow his last name is the same as my middle name) Wiersma (Did I just get an award for being excellent at something??????)."

I hesitate to tell that part of the story because I don't want to sound self-glorifying. In my mind, I still picture a few gifted classmates whom I think should have received that award. But that isn't the point. The point is that God took a man who thought he would be the worst of the seminary students in his class and gave him a pat on the back as if to say once again, "I told you I have this figured out." God wanted me to complete seminary and have confidence in what was next. He made it happen. All things are possible with God.

This book is another example of God's work. The idea stirred within me for some time. I found ample excuses to justify why I couldn't and shouldn't even try to put a book together. Once again, I came to the end of myself and the urge to say that I can't. I've surrendered myself in obedience to write it and fully expect God to use it as He sees fit.

Can a scatter-brained, middle-aged prison pastor actually author a book anyone would want to read? Well, you made it this far. I've learned that if God wants us to, we can. You and I can do all things (in His will) through Christ who gives me (us) strength.

Reflection Questions

- Have you heard others misuse the phrase, "All things are possible with God?" If so, how?
- Have you ever witnessed God do something incredible that you'd formerly thought was impossible? If so, what were the results of the miracle?
- Why do you think God prefers to use unlikely and reluctant candidates like Moses and Peter to do His work?
- Read Philippians 4:11-13. How does considering the two prior verses (bringing in context) help you understand Philippians 4:13?

"If you need freedom or saving,
He's a prison shaking Savior.
If you got chains,
He's a chain breaker."

— *Lyrics from Zach Williams' song,*
"Chainbreaker"

9

Freedom For
The Prisoner

It's tough to choose between two good things. We've all stared at a menu, trying to decide between two equally appetizing entrée options.

A bacon cheeseburger is a safe option, but the picture of the stir fry seems so appealing. It stinks when you order one thing, your friend or spouse orders the other, and theirs comes out looking fabulous, leaving you in regret. But, of course, you can just order what they did the next time you're in that restaurant.

As our seminary years drew to a close, Ruth and I tried to discern our next steps. We knew the importance of the decisions ahead. Multiple churches inquired about my availability to pastor their flock. But even as I preached and enjoyed getting to know believers in these various congregations, I knew my calling wasn't to a traditional setting.

I had already interned with Cornerstone Prison Church in Sioux Falls, which was a great experience. Ruth and I also left a good portion of our hearts in Haiti as a result of multiple mission trips there (more on that later).

We were faced with two excellent options, unsure which one God wanted us to pursue.

Fittingly, for someone called to reach out into brokenness, my life verses are Psalm 40:1-3: *"I waited patiently for the LORD; he inclined to me and heard my cry. He drew me up from the pit of destruction, out of the miry bog, and set my feet upon a rock, making my steps secure. He put a new song in my mouth, a song of praise to our God. Many will see and fear and put their trust in the LORD."*

God had indeed pulled me out of a pit, set me on the rock of His Word, and guided my steps. Now it was time to figure out where we would *"sing"* our "new song" by which many "will see" and fear God and put their trust in Him.

Having test-driven prison ministry already, Ruth and I spent a month in Haiti the January before seminary graduation. During that time, we lived on a missionary compound, seeking the Lord to discern whether this was our calling. It was an exceedingly challenging and powerful time. One night, I was really asking God for discernment. I didn't demand a sign, but I made it clear if there was an angel that wasn't really busy at the moment, I was ready for a message from above.

No angel appeared. But, opening my eyes, I immediately noticed that light shining through the multi-paned window of the room where I was sleeping, created an image of prison bars on the wall. The shadow also held the shape of three crosses. I knew the Lord had spoken. We returned to the States, confident about our next step in ministry.

People react strangely when you announce you've chosen (or in our case have been called to) a future inside a prison. A cement truck operator who had delivered many loads of concrete during my construction days swore at me in disbelief when I told him.

One man who heard me speak came up to me afterward with his plan for my life. I could pastor his church and do my prison thing on the side. He looked at me like I had two heads when I said prison ministry was to be my main focus and, perhaps, I could preach at his church on the side.

Years before, when I was a corrections officer, I built rapport with an older lifer by the name of Jimmy. Our friendship was mainly due to the fact we both enjoyed working with horses. It always gave us something to talk about. When I resigned at the prison, it was difficult because I wouldn't have an opportunity to speak with him anymore.

On my final day, I said something that turned out to be rather prophetic. I said I believed I would return to prison one day in a different role. Believe me, the idea of being a pastor was not on the radar then. Thankfully I didn't have to catch a felony to make those words ring true either.

It was approximately 10 years later, in 2011, that I returned to the South Dakota State Prison system to plant a prison church.

Some will never understand how people like Ruth and I can set aside the realization that many of the men we work with have done terrible things to hurt others. As one man put it, "We aren't in prison for jaywalking." I've had peace about working in prison ministry ever since God gave me some insight during one of the first times I volunteered to do ministry in prison.

I was sitting at a table, inmates sitting all around me. The thought hit me that every one of these men was probably hated by at least one person, and for good reason. Should I hate them too?

That question rolled around in my mind. Suddenly, in my mind's eye, I saw a young boy in a closet, crying as violent and hateful things were happening outside of it. At that moment, God asked me, "Can you hate this boy?" My answer: "Of course not! Look at him, he's scared and just a boy. He needs love, not hate!"

Then I saw the boy as a man, acting out in the same kind of violent ways he'd experienced as a child. What I heard the Lord say is, "Neither can you hate this man. He too needs love and not hatred."

The message coming from that lesson is that a felon often starts out as a victim. It is God's love that can redeem them and break the cycle.

In August 2011, I launched my first Bible study at Mike Durfee State Prison in Springfield, South Dakota. It was one way to share God's love. We started with four men. Before long, there were dozens of men attending, and our small study room was bursting at the seams.

I designated a team of five inmates with whom I already had a working relationship to form a committee that could gather and seek the Lord's direction for the ministry. As a group, we chose the name Living Stone Prison Church. In 2012 we were able to begin meeting once a month for worship.

The chapel space we used was quickly packed with inmates eager to hear a word from the Lord that would help them in their current situations.

By March 2012, I was ordained and officially recognized as a specialized pastor catering to the needs of the Mike Durfee State Prison. Ordination was another essential step that affirmed what God had called us to do.

Church was hard for me as I was growing up. I had to sit still, be quiet for an entire hour, just waiting for the pastor to say, "AMEN!" and end the service so I could escape. Honestly, It was probably the most challenging hour of my week.

Now I was a pastor. I didn't want our services to be boring. As a kid, even in church, I wanted to be on the move. Turns out I had the right idea about church: it SHOULD be on the move. If not within the church building, then certainly outside it. We are the Body of Christ, and He likes to be on the go, searching for the lost.

I hold to my opinion that a weary religious gathering is not what God has in mind for His flock. In our worship services, as long as it is God-glorifying, we provide opportunities for congregants to use their gifts of poetry, playwriting, sermon presentation, testimony, songwriting (even rap music at times), etc. Sometimes these efforts don't go so well, but Living Stone is a gathering where men can fail and try again.

We offer a place of Grace where we all can learn at the feet of Jesus and serve Him together. Prison ministry in this modern day of mass incarceration is a much-needed mission of the church. We cherish the opportunity we've been given.

We are a congregation of Baptists, Reformers, Methodists, Charismatics, Catholics, Lutherans, Mennonites and probably any other denomination I didn't mention. We've also had people like Mormons and Muslims consistently check us out. Seekers attend service weekly.

We use the Bible as our guide for worship and service and regularly celebrate the sacraments of communion and baptism. I like to say we "major on the majors," meaning we cling to the sacred truths of the Bible, emphasizing that all who believe in Jesus are saved by the Blood of the Lamb and guided by the Holy Spirit. We avoid putting up strict denominational borders.

As a youth, there was a particular Sunday I did get excited about. I loved attending services when missionaries spoke. They told stories of how God was at work in their mission fields. They sounded like stories I read about in the Bible, and that was thrilling. I drank in their tales, longing to see for myself the conversions and miraculous happenings they described.

I loved the trips Ruth and I made to Haiti as we experienced first-hand God's power at work in a foreign land. But I also learned it was not necessary to leave America to witness God's power unleashed. Any place there is openness to the Gospel and guidance of the Holy Spirit is an area fertile for God to move.

God planted within Ruth and me a missionary's heart to reach out to other races and cultures. Although the Mike Durfee State Prison population is made up of many white Midwest folks like us, prison has a culture all its own. God has continued feeding our desire to minister to and with people coming from far different cultural backgrounds.

Over the years, our prison congregation has included men from Burma, South Africa, Guatemala, Somalia, El Salvador, the Congo, China, Egypt, Sudan, Haiti, Russia, various Indian reservations and the list goes on and on.

I've distributed Bibles in multiple languages, and we've had men that probably didn't understand much of what was said during the service. They came anyway because they still experienced the presence of the Savior.

At the beginning of our calling, Ruth and I needed God's revelation to help us decide between two valuable mission fields. He led us into the prison but has still fed our passion for foreign missions. In fact, many foreign inmates are sent back to their country of origin, where they have opportunities to proclaim the Gospel to their family and communities.

We say, along with King David, *"Delight yourself in the LORD, and he will give you the desires of your heart* (Psalm 37:4)."

In recent days, an inmate I'll call Bashir joined our congregation. He's from a country and family where Muslim extremism is the rule. But as he spent time in Mike Durfee State Prison, he observed Christians and saw something in them he wanted for himself.

Bashir came to Living Stone services and asked the mature Christians in his housing unit a lot of questions. Eventually, Bashir decided to follow Jesus, and we baptized him at our weekly service. He realizes it's very possible that he will be deported back to a country that will be hostile to his response to the Gospel. But he told me he isn't going to turn from following Jesus. Given the opportunity, Bashir plans to reach his family with the Good News about the Savior.

I'm impressed by this man's faith. Stories like these are what keep me going in what can be a most challenging ministry.

Many complain about the current situation in America, with our prisons bursting at the seams. To use a quote originating from China, where the church is persecuted and yet growing: "It is better to light a candle than to curse the darkness." In other words, rather than complaining about a dark situation, do what you can to bring light to it.

God has granted a man who was highly reluctant to accept his calling the opportunity to be a light in the prison system of South Dakota. And I've born witness to how The Light of the World (John 8:12) has pierced the lives of many who had formerly walked in darkness.

Reflection Questions

- Have you ever had to decide between two good options that could alter the course of your life's direction? How did you find the answer? How did it turn out?
- Read Psalm 37:4. Has this verse come alive in your life? If so, how?
- What do you think of this quote? "It is better to light a candle than to curse the darkness." How might you apply that thought to your life?
- Why do you think God's power is often more evident in dark and difficult situations?

"There is no neutral ground in the universe; every square inch, every split second is claimed by God and counter-claimed by Satan."

— C.S. Lewis

10

BEWARE OF
THE SWAT TEAM

If you've watched any of the prison reality shows they play on television today, you've probably seen a cell entry team at work. As a corrections officer, I was part of such a team, multiple times. These teams are called in as a last resort to situations in which an inmate is out of control, disrupting his area and refusing to listen to instructions.

As a team, we dressed up in protective clothing. The lead man (sometimes me) carried a shield. We apprehended and removed the man from the cell or area he was in, shackling his feet and arms. The idea was to stop the threat before the rebellion became contagious.

This often worked, but I do recall a time when our team had to extract inmates from an entire section of the maximum security area. We regained control, but it wasn't easy, with so many men giving themselves to chaos.

At the time, a man named Jackson wreaked a lot of havoc and often required the attention of the cell entry team. He now resides in MDSP. Recently we sat in my office and talked, which I found inspiring. Two men who were formerly on the opposite side of a cell entry extraction are now able to have a peaceful conversation. He admitted that the chaos in his life back then was fed by an identification with the forces of darkness. Jackson has since surrendered himself to the Light of the World (Jesus) and has become a fruit-bearing Christian, a far different life than the dark, rebellious existence of his former days. He has no further interest in causing disturbances within the prison.

If there's a disturbance outside of prison, a SWAT (Special Weapons and Tactics) team may be called in to squelch the situation. I, for one, wouldn't like to be the subject of a SWAT team intervention. They're highly trained to use whatever force necessary to put things back in order. I'm happy to stay off their radar as I'm sure their special weapons and tactics would result in a world of hurt.

But there is a SWAT team that has attacked me on multiple occasions. Satan, the author of chaos. He has a team of his own. It's important to recognize this because, once we're serious about serving the Lord, the devil gets really serious about getting in our way. This is where a team of dark, demon distractors (1 Timothy 4:1) and accusers (Revelation 12:10) are sent on a mission to try and stop members of God's team from reaching their potential for spreading the Good News about Jesus.

We will experience resistance to some degree any time we step out in Jesus' name. I believe this chapter is significant because some Christians can give up rather quickly when they don't understand spiritual warfare and how to respond when they experience kick-back on something they feel called to do.

The devil knows he's lost the war to gain control of us when we have Jesus as our Savior and Lord. That doesn't mean he stops fighting battles to keep us fearful and less effective for the Kingdom. His SWAT team doesn't prevent disturbances, it creates them.

I break down Satan's team with this acronym: Satan–Will–Attempt–Terrorism (SWAT). Satan will throw fear and doubt at us in any way he can to sabotage God's plan for our life. Terrorism is an act of intimidation and/or violence in an attempt to induce life-altering fear. The perfect love of Jesus casts out fear because He has taken our punishment on the cross (1 John 4:13-18).

Satan's goal is to terrorize Christians into thinking that they're still unworthy and/or in danger of hellfire. If we buy into the lie, it holds us back from reaching out to others in Christ's love because of shame. This could mean sabotaging our life's calling or undermining a God-appointed event or task.

Satan wants us stuck, imprisoned and held at bay by the attacks of his SWAT team. It's important to note that Jesus has already won the war on the cross. However, if we are easily discouraged, the SWAT team will keep us in a prison in which we are unable to fight in battles that still remain (think POW).

I don't like it, but I've learned to expect attacks anytime Living Stone Prison Church has a special event that will be used to powerfully advance God's Kingdom. Satan doesn't like to lose territory. He often causes division among those organizing an event. He tries to cause speakers and/or musicians to question their involvement.

These attacks come in many forms. The best advice I have for those about to step out in faith is to be flexible, have a plan B in case things don't go as expected (and typically something won't). But, here's the deal: if you are acting in obedience to God, He will use you and what you're doing, flaws and all.

One August day, during our Freedom Feed event, a severe thunderstorm hit us just as I was welcoming the afternoon group. Not only that, the storm hit just as a solar eclipse was occurring above the clouds (it looked like something out of a Stephen King movie).

A staff member shouted that everyone must go to the chow hall. We retreated as the rain beat down, soaking all of us. The day was ruined, or so we thought. But our event speakers—Lifelight's Alan Green, Josh Brewer and, Christian rapper Bobby Bugatii—were undisturbed by the interruption. As heavy rain beat down on the metal roof of the chow hall, they talked over all the noise, giving testimony of what God had done in their lives and the power of the cross.

Despite the chaotic circumstances, many inmates responded to the Gospel message. It became clear that God's plan B worked better than we could have imagined.

It's not just me who has noticed the relationship between God using someone and the SWAT attacks. Loretta, editor of this book and her husband, Al, have gone into prison to teach marriage classes. Ironically, they found they often had their worst fights on the way to teach the men about having a Christ-centered marriage. God still used their efforts, but they began to question their own credibility. Eventually, they recognized what was happening and prayerfully and intentionally kept the devil's team at bay.

The powers of darkness try to sabotage major life choices in their favor whenever they can. My mother is a second-career nurse who started nursing classes in her mid 40's. Over the years, her patients have benefited greatly from having a godly woman care for them during their time of greatest need. Mom completed one semester in nursing school before she and dad were married. She hoped to continue her schooling, but they had me instead. Great choice! The world can't thank you enough, Mom! ☺

In middle age, the nursing bug bit Mom once again. This time she decided to go for it. She had to pass a pretest to pursue a nursing degree. She arranged to carpool with another nursing candidate to travel to a facility offering the exam. On the appointed day, the other woman was a no-show. Mom really contemplated going home, thinking maybe it was a sign that the whole idea was crazy.

However, she found the courage to go anyway, opening the door to a God-glorifying career as a nurse. At her recent retirement party, her supervisor called her career a *"calling,"* which it was.

I believe the carpool situation on that day so many years ago was a spiritual attack meant to discourage her from doing God's will. It was thwarted by mom's godly determination, and no doubt some angelic soldiers.

I can tell you the devil gave me his best shot just after I was called into ministry. A group of friends from my Bible study invited me to help them put on a Brothers in Blue prison ministry weekend in Iowa. Since I had worked in prison, I was excited to go back, especially as an ambassador of the Savior of the world.

As the day we were to leave approached, I was hit by the SWAT team of darkness. As I tried to sleep the night before our departure, anxious, racing thoughts hit me at 100 miles per hour. I heard thoughts about not being worthy to minister, accusations of having no idea what to do when I got into the prison. The SWAT team told me to stay home since my involvement was bound to be a disaster.

To be honest, if I could have thought of a good excuse to get out of going, I would have. But the group of servants who invited me was coming to pick me up in the wee hours of the morning, so we would reach the prison on time. If God hadn't brought me into that group, I could have missed my calling.

Once again, God met me in that prison and helped me effectively encourage inmates through the Gospel message. The resistance I felt was nothing compared to the power of God I experienced during those three days.

Since that weekend, I've spent countless hours in prisons proclaiming the Good News about Jesus. There was good reason for Satan to attempt to keep me out of the prison systems. Thankfully, God's got his own team and weapons, both offensive and defensive, that are far greater than the enemy's.

Ephesians Chapter 6 is a great passage to study as it pertains to what we're talking about in this chapter: Satan's attacks and our defense. Ephesians 6:10–12 says; *"Finally, be strong in the Lord and in the strength of his might. Put on the whole armor of God, that you may be able to stand against the schemes of the devil. For we do not wrestle against flesh and blood, but against the rulers, against the authorities, against the cosmic powers over this present darkness, against the spiritual forces of evil in the heavenly places."*

You see, we might think our struggle is against the man who took a verbal shot at us or perhaps the family member who discourages us from moving forward in our faith. But truth be told, there is an unseen cosmic power of darkness. It uses flesh and blood humans, and anything else it can muster, to come against God's plans.

Even though I've had this book on my heart for years, in the early stages of writing I became distracted and discouraged by conflict with someone close to me. Suddenly, God opened my eyes to what was really going on and who was working to sabotage what God was asking me to do (Satan Will Attempt Terrorism). I reconciled with that person and regained my focus to continue with the task at hand.

When we read stories of Biblical figures like Abraham and Sarah, Joseph, Deborah, King David, Peter, and Paul, we see narratives of people who ran into all sorts of pestilence and resistance. Still, they pressed on to do God's will. Forces of evil tried their best to bring confusion to God's plan, yet all these individuals played a role in bringing the message of salvation to the world. These heroes of the faith didn't experience the prosperity gospel, they lived out the perseverance gospel, the good news that God walked with them through their joys and difficulties to fulfill their calling.

Satan's SWAT team tried but couldn't stop God from wreaking havoc upon the kingdom of darkness. The above paragraphs can be applied by two different groups of people. Perhaps, for some time, you've been obediently serving God in whatever way He asks. I'm sure you've experienced both personal attacks and spiritual attacks on your work. This doesn't mean you're a failure. In fact, it likely means you're succeeding in glorifying God and are therefore a target. Feel free to give me that reminder if you ever see that I need it.

Or perhaps you're someone who has dabbled in serving the Lord in one way or another, experienced resistance and decided to back off because of it. I'm here to tell you that you won't succeed in any type of special task or calling God would have you do without feeling the heat and finding strength in Christ to continue. Expect attacks, but know you are NEVER alone in the battle.

Reflection Questions

- Have you ever experienced an attack from the devil's SWAT team? If so, how did it turn out?
- Read Ephesians 6:10-18. How can we be intentional about putting on the armor of God?
- Read 1 John 4:18. Why do you think perfect love casts out fear?
- Why do you think God allows Satan to attack us? What can we learn from such battles?

*"If you want to lift yourself up,
lift up someone else."*

— Booker T. Washington

11

OF FREEDOM
AND STARFISHES

It's guaranteed, if you follow the Spirit long enough, He'll take you places you didn't even know you wanted to go. The year after we received the call into ministry was the first time Ruth and I went on a mission trip to Haiti. We had never visited a foreign country before, but Ruth's parents invited us to encounter the tiny Caribbean country where they'd been going for several years. What we experienced there was life-altering.

We traveled with a group from Hope Missions Outreach based in Bethany, Missouri, led by Bob and Sharon Johnson. Once again, Ruth and I felt God set us up to learn and grow from this new adventure. The Haitian Christians we met during the trip were beautiful souls who exhibited joy in Christ despite (and perhaps because of) their struggles with poverty. Our world view was forever changed as we walked through their villages and met Haitian people, young and old, who lived lives that were so much different than ours.

We were challenged by one group leader, Mike, to share the Gospel with those who hadn't heard. My nerves tingled as I followed his instruction. I was amazed at the response of listeners as the Holy Spirit brought forth men and women who were ready to surrender to the One who gave His life for them.

Ruth and I wondered what we might do with the love we now had for our new Haitian brothers and sisters. The challenges of Haiti were far too great for us to answer them all. So, how might we respond to all we were experiencing?

Our answer came in the form of a fable that's popular in Christian circles; I know it merely as the *"Starfish Story."*

"One day, an old man was walking along a beach littered with thousands of starfish that had been washed ashore by the high tide. As he walked, he came upon a young boy who was eagerly throwing the starfish back into the ocean, one by one. Puzzled, the man looked at the boy and asked what he was doing. Without looking up from his task, the boy simply replied, 'I'm saving these starfish, sir.'

"The old man chuckled aloud. 'Son, there are thousands of starfish and only one of you. What difference can you make?'

The boy picked up a starfish, gently tossed it into the water and turning to the man, said, 'I made a difference to that one!'"

There are over 8 million people in Haiti, many of whom could use a hand up to better their situation. We needed God to give us some direction.

During our first trip there we met a teenager named Wiliamson who would become our "starfish." I made a rookie mistake on that trip. I was walking in the village of Titanyen (pronounced TEA-TY-ANN) while holding a bag of small plastic animals. In America, children would have paid me no mind, but the Haitian children were drawn to me as if I had a bagful of the newest iPads to distribute.

Jesus once said, *"Let the little children come to me and do not hinder them, for to such belongs the kingdom of heaven* (Matthew 19:14)." I do want to be like Jesus, but it literally got to the point that I was being mobbed and couldn't even walk enough to keep up with the group. It's as if all the heavenly little children were conspiring to hinder Jason from getting anywhere.† Wiliamson, watching the whole thing transpire, spoke English well and took pity on me.

When he asked if I wanted him to help, I took him up on his offer and handed him the bag. The children immediately diverted their efforts from me and to my new Haitian friend. Wiliamson wisely opened the bag of animals and scattered them like seeds, which sent the kids scrambling to find one.

After being saved from the mob of renegade village children, I wanted to know more about the young man who'd come up with the rescue plan. Wiliamson invited me to see his house, which had four walls but no roof. When it rained, he became wet and cold, and the powerful Haitian sun baked the home

---

† 40 Haitian children have the power of a small tornado, take my word for it!

whenever there were no clouds.

I learned that Wiliamson's father had abandoned the family, and his mother had moved into the mountains, leaving Wiliamson to look after his younger siblings. Our heart went out to him. When we returned to the States, we found someone willing to donate the necessary funds to put a roof on the young Haitian man's home to make it livable.

In the years that followed, Ruth and I continued to get to know Wiliamson and his family as we traveled to Haiti several more times. He interpreted for us in the villages and even taught me some Haitian words and phrases.†

One day we learned the government was going to take Wiliamson's land away because his father had never really purchased the property, just built a house on it. Once again, God led us to someone who donated funds to purchase the land in Wiliamson's name legally.

We were also able to help him with schooling and eventually, job placement at a medical mission, which gave him the means to take care of his family and send his brothers to school.

Eventually, Wiliamson fell in love with a pretty physician's assistant by the name of Rachel, who had traveled to Haiti from North Carolina. The two were married a few years ago and currently reside in Charlotte.

While Wiliamson's American dream was realized, this

† "Bondye beni ou mwen zanmi" translates to "God bless you my friend!"

"starfish" has not forgotten where he came from. The young couple has started a non-profit called Higher Hope Connect Ministries which is active in the village of Titanyen. They provide food, education, jobs, biblical guidance, etc. to Wiliamson's former neighbors. The land where his Haitian home sits is now being transformed into a center for ministry for the villagers.

Recently Ruth and I traveled to Charlotte to visit Rachel and Wiliamson. We've already begun collaborating on how we might do ministry together in the future. This story is still being written.

The application I'd like to make here is that God is not asking any of us to try and save the world (Jesus already did that). But if every one of God's people reached out to make a difference for one person at a time, I'm convinced we, with God's guidance, could once again turn this world upside down (Acts 17:6).

But, don't be surprised if God takes your obedience in something small and expands on it over time. As far as Haiti is concerned, we started with Wiliamson. But our family has since sponsored multiple children, and we've been involved in building projects, feeding programs, and leading groups to experience Haiti for themselves.

The inmates of Living Stone Prison Church have also donated to provide an education for three orphans and have provided food and Bibles for many a Haitian soul.

Some might think that, in prison, the opportunity to reach out with the love of God is limited because of one's captivity. This might be partially true; the incarcerated person cannot go out to reach their fellow man. But, simply put, they don't have to go anywhere to have ample opportunity to reach out to others in Christ's love. The penal system sends plenty of people in their direction.

One of our first Living Stone inside (inmate) board members used to pray God would send him a cell mate who needed to hear the Gospel. When that person arrived, he was happy to share Jesus with them.

There are also men within our congregation who have earned biblical degrees during their stay at MDSP. Terry completed a counseling degree from Moody Bible Institute and put it to good use inside the walls, working with Prison Fellowship to prepare fellow inmates for re-entry into their communities.

Nolan earned his Master's in Divinity and Doctorate in ministry while serving time. He is using his education to teach other inmates the truth of God's Word and plans to continue to do so for the rest of his stay. Ray has helped countless numbers of men earn their GED (General Educational Development). This is one way he has served God as the years of his sentence tick down.

Jose is an avid weightlifter who likes to reach out to the rougher crowd (renegade starfish) in prison, challenging them to give Jesus a chance. Multiple men who have done so have now been drawn in by God's Grace. Inmates who pray and wait for the opportunity to use their prison sentence for God's glory are very successful at doing just that.

It's been long recognized that fatherlessness is a primary factor leading to incarceration. That fact gives birth to another opportunity for the mature in faith. Mark is an older inmate I've known for some time. Over the years, I've witnessed how he mentors John, a younger inmate whose father has been absent or an inconsistent presence for most of John's life.

In the prison culture, there's a hesitation to accept help from anyone. The thought is, "If I get something from you, what do you expect of me?" In Mark's case, he took an opportunity to be a light to someone in the generation below him. God gave him a chance to serve within the prison, and I've watched John grow in faith and maturity, primarily because of Mark's diligence.

John has found the courage to put together scriptural teachings he's shared publicly at our worship services and steadily contributes during our Bible studies. That would not have happened without the encouragement of a positive male role model. Once again, this story highlights the power of reaching out to one "starfish" (made a difference to that one).

Ecclesiastes 4:9–10 says this: *Two are better than one, because they have a good reward for their toil. For if they fall, one will lift up his fellow. But woe to him who is alone when he falls and has not another to lift him up!*

We all need the type of friend who can pick us up when we are down, who can toil with us, so we get the job done more efficiently. We need that kind of friend, so let's be that kind of friend.

Who might the Lord be asking you to walk alongside? You

may be surprised at what God will do when you simply take time to encourage someone who needs it! This world is big and broken; somebody needs what you have to offer.

Reflection Questions

- What problems do you see around you that are overwhelming? What is one thing you could do to help alleviate the problem?
- Do you think the world could be turned upside down in a positive way if every Christian reached out in love to one person? Why or why not?
- Why do you think God usually gives a small vision at first and expands on it later?
- Why do you think many Christians miss opportunities to share Christ's love? What could be done so more of God's people develop an active faith?

*"Sin came through the pride of Lucifer
and salvation came through
the humility of Jesus."*

— *Zac Poonen*

12

THE PRISON OF PRIDE

Generally speaking, I pride myself on not being prideful. (Oh crud, that came out wrong!) What I mean is that one benefit of having a learning disability and experiencing an anxiety disorder is that, in most situations, it's not hard for me to place others on a higher plane than myself. This includes my interactions with inmates. But I must confess, I have some obvious flaws in my desire to live humbly.

One of my main issues is that I'm horribly competitive. This means if you start playing pin the tail on the donkey and invite me to participate, I'll either decline or try to beat you with everything I've got. And don't think I won't practice at home beforehand. (I told you it was terrible!)

As much as I enjoy my own victories, I'm far worse as it pertains to my kids and their achievements. I'm proud of my kids. They've all overachieved, especially since they're infused with my DNA.† I'll pick on my son Levi since, as I write this, he's closing out his senior year of high school.

I worried a lot when Levi was young that he was ADHD. I feared he might drop out of high school and become a rebel. Nothing could be further from the truth. He gets good grades, is very active in his youth group, was chosen as Homecoming king, and has an academic and football scholarship at a Christian college. Pretty incredible, considering I didn't even complete my senior year.

Our children will undoubtedly face future trials and temptations, but it's clear that, as God has redeemed my story, our children are part of that redemption.

As I said, I'm proud of my kids. The problem comes when I think a coach, or perhaps a ref or teacher, has slighted one of them. In those situations, I can instantly become a prideful moron.

Years ago, after letting an official have it from the sidelines, my own dad reminded me that I was a pastor. (YIKES—WAKE UP CALL!) It's good to be proud of your children and desire to see them do well. Far too often though, I've been guilty of wanting to see my kids do well with little or no regard for others (you know, the people Jesus asks me to love in John 13:34) involved in situations that trigger these flare-ups.

The first step to repentance and recovery is admitting you have a problem. I've done that. For this particular type of pride, I believe I'm in remission and healing.

†   There I go with the low self-esteem thing again.

I don't like the feeling I get when acting out in pride. That makes sense when considering what scripture says: *"One's pride will bring him low, but he who is lowly in spirit will obtain honor (Proverbs 29:23)."*

The original Hebrew word translated as pride in English implies being puffed up and arrogant. That type of pride doesn't look good on people. It's also another type of prison.

I think we can make a distinction between healthy pride and toxic pride. If I say I'm proud to be an American, it could just mean I'm patriotic. But if I say I'm proud to be an American and, in my heart, consider every other nation and people to be inferior, then I have a toxic pride issue that needs to be addressed.

Healthy pride is a good thing regarding family, country, communities, etc. But pride becomes a problem when we elevate ourselves or our situation to a place where we look down on others.

The worst kind of pride is the haughty type that causes us to believe we can handle anything that comes our way without recognizing our dependence on God.

Jesus made it clear that self-reliance is not an option for His followers. He said in Luke 9:23-24: *"If anyone would come after me, let him deny himself and take up his cross daily and follow me. For whoever would save his life will lose it, but whoever loses his life for my sake will save it."*

Followers of Jesus are to lose themselves in Him, denying their own agenda in favor of His superior plan. The late pastor and theologian, A. W. Pink, put it this way: "Taking up my 'cross' means a life voluntarily surrendered to God."

The first essential move of faith is surrendering and beginning to deny oneself those things that are apart from God. Pride is one of those things.

Probably the most recognizable verse of many in scripture that speaks on this subject is Proverbs 16:18: *"Pride goes before destruction, and a haughty spirit before a fall."*

Friends, I have witnessed this verse played out in many lives. The type of pride this passage talks about is the arrogant, self-exalting type. In fact, pride is often the underlying issue that sends a person to prison.

I know a man who struggled to pay his bills. He told me he had family and friends who would have helped him out. But his pride tempted him to handle the situation himself. As a result, he committed armed robbery and spent many years in prison. It was a *"pride fall"* for sure.

Other inmates have experienced pride in the area of entitlement. They felt they deserved something that wasn't theirs, so they took it. That type of pride leads to theft, rape, murder, and a host of other felonies.

But the prison of selfish pride is one we can live in, right in our own community or living room, for that matter. Pride can imprison us because, when we are under its influence, we will never be free in Christ. James 4:6-7 says this: *"But He (God) gives more grace. Therefore, it says, 'God opposes the proud but gives grace to the humble.' Submit yourselves therefore to God. Resist the devil, and he will flee from you."*

Part of resisting the devil is to resist pride. God opposes the proud because they think they don't need Him. What each one of us does need is Grace. We need Grace because we all mess up in our desire (or lack thereof) to do God's will. I need Grace as I struggle to keep my highly competitive nature from bringing out the worst in me again.

God gives Grace to the humble because they are receptive to it. They understand they cannot do it on their own. They rely on their need for a Savior.

If you've read the Gospels of the New Testament, you know Jesus was always at odds with the religious group called the Pharisees. These Jewish leaders were very prideful and considered themselves the cream of the crop. Jesus saw right through the facade and into their cold black hearts.

The Pharisees carried themselves with haughtiness because they felt they had earned their way into Heaven, both through their stellar religious practices and the fact that they were descendants of Abraham.

I'll be honest. I sometimes come across individuals from churches who, like the Pharisees, think they have it all together. They really believe they are "THE church,"† the one God has anointed above all others with a unique brand of religion.

When I find myself around such people, I'm friendly, but generally avoid theological discussions. By nature, I'm non-confrontational. And in my experience, no amount of talking

---

† I think every geographic area has a church like this. The denomination varies.

can change their mind, only God can do that.

Jesus however, had no problem calling out the Pharisees. For instance, look what he said to them in the second part of Matthew 21:31: *"Truly, I say to you, the tax collectors and the prostitutes go into the kingdom of God before you."* (No reason to wonder why they killed him!)

You see, this is the perfect example of what we are talking about in this chapter. The Pharisees rejected the words of John the Baptist, which proclaimed Jesus as the way to righteousness (Matthew 21:32). They were awaiting the Messiah, but now that He had appeared, they refused to acknowledge Him. In effect, the Pharisees said, "No!" to God out of pride. They thought they were better than His Son!

On the flip side, thieving tax collectors and sinful prostitutes embraced the idea of a Savior. They changed their mind about the way they were living and humbly accepted the righteousness Jesus offered. They knew plumb well they could never achieve it on their own. Let me set aside my non-confrontational personality for a minute and say this: if you think your membership to a specific church/denomination or your ability to follow a religious code has earned you right standing with God and/or a place in Heaven, you're not grasping the reality of the Gospel.

I'll even be so bold as to say this: the inmates of Mike Durfee State Prison are entering the Kingdom of Heaven ahead of you. I made the statement in the intro that I believe "many of the inmates in my prison congregation have more freedom than many people on the 'outs.'" The reason for this isn't that I'm such a good pastor. The reason is many inmates tend to really embrace the fact that they cannot do life on their own. They look to the Savior, who offers them freedom in His Grace, and they humble themselves in sweet surrender.

Like the tax collectors and prostitutes of Jesus' day, many inmates live in liberty simply because they trust in what God has offered them through the cross. They know they can't rely on themselves.

I've told many people I appreciate the level of honesty I experience in prison. I find that the majority of the men coming to me for biblical counsel and prayer are real about the issues in their life. They know their life is broken and in need of repair. Many people in the outside church are rather good at hiding their brokenness, so others don't know. Sadly, this often means their problems go unresolved because of pride.

Masking our pain is one way in which our pride can become a prison. Jesus sees right through our facade, recognizes what's really going on inside. Until a person relinquishes the idea that they can make their own way in life, they will not experience the power of God applied to their life.

Jim Logan, who has served as a biblical restoration counselor for decades, puts it this way: "When Satan succumbed to pride, God shoved him out of Heaven. When I allow pride in my life, God shoves me away, as it were. He says, 'I'll take My power off of your life.' What will happen then? I'll fall."

Pride comes before a fall because we were not created to

be self-sustaining. We were created to live in fellowship with and be dependent on our Creator.

I recall a time, early in my prison ministry ventures, when an inmate called me and those with me that day, a bunch of "sissies."† I guess, in his mind, because we recognized dependence on a Savior, we were weak. In my experience, the opposite has been true. Since the day I began following the Holy Spirit instead of my own inclinations, my courage and boldness in Christ have given me the strength to do things I'd never imagined I'd take on.

I think of David who is famous for defeating a 9-foot Philistine named Goliath with just a sling and a stone (1 Samuel 17). The guy who would become Israel's most celebrated king was a man of great courage and strength, a mighty warrior who struck fear in the hearts of his enemies. But by some people's standards, he was also a *"sissy."*

Check out what David says in Psalm 20:7: *"Some trust in chariots and some in horses, but we trust in the name of the LORD our God."* You see, David was strong and courageous because he was surrendered to God. Whenever he let his pride get in the way of his relationship with the Almighty, he quickly learned from his error and turned back to the Lord.

Sadly, even ministry leaders can succumb to pride. And some are not receptive to correction.

Years ago I attended a conference where a pastor talked

† Let the record show that I refrained from calling the man a "big dummy head" in return.

with great emotion about his mentor, who had recently failed morally. The man testified he had noticed the older pastor getting too friendly with a young woman in his church. When questioned about it, the mentor said it was nobody else's concern because he answered only to God.

Turns out, he wasn't paying attention to God's guidance, either. He proceeded to get into a sinful relationship that left things in shambles. It could all have been avoided had the pastor accepted correction and been God-reliant instead of self-reliant.

This is what Paul was getting at in 1 Corinthians 10:12: *"Therefore let anyone who thinks that he stands take heed lest he fall."* When pride wells up inside us, we must catch it and repent lest it becomes a stumbling block and a prison in our life.

If you've been incarcerated by your pride (or still are), be reminded that you were never supposed to do things on your own (1 Corinthians 10:13). Escape can be found on your knees.

Reflection Questions

- Why do you think pride can cause so many problems?
- Why is humility so much more desirable than pride in a friend?
- Have you ever experienced a "pride fall?" If so, what did you learn from it?
- Why do so many church folks hide their weaknesses?
- Do you believe faith in Jesus is a trait of weakness or strength? Why?

Jason and Ruth were married on September 27, 1996. Ruth stuck around but Jason's hair didn't.

At Louisiana's Angola prison, Jason stepped behind the bars for a few minutes.

Jason Wiersma
and Burl Cain
(former Angola warden).

Jason and Ruth Wiersma in
Mike Durfee State Prison Chapel.

Wiliamson (center) and Jason (right)
sharing the Gospel in Haiti.

*"The key to forgiving others
is to stop focusing on what they did
to you and start focusing on
what God did for you."*

— Max Lucado

13

THE FELONY OF UNFORGIVENESS

In 2018 my dad left earth for his eternal home. I would have so loved to have had him around longer, but I'm thankful for the years I was blessed in having a father.

Through my work in the prison, I'm acutely aware of the effect fatherlessness can have on a person. Those who grow up without a father are far more likely to end up incarcerated. I'm thankful that, when I went through my rebellious teenage years, I had my dad to call me out when I needed it and provide an example of what a godly man was like.

My dad was forgiving, and that's a good thing because my brothers and I needed a lot of it. I clearly recall a night I was under the influence of far too many fluid ounces of "barley pop."† Being strapped for cash earlier that evening, I figured

† In layman's terms, that's beer.

a quick swipe of a few bucks worth of quarters from my dad's dresser would help pay for that night's essential supplies (nicotine and alcohol).

At the close of the night, when I came home, all I wanted was to sleep it off. But when I walked into the house, dad sat at the table with a Bible. He asked if I had taken his money. I lied and said, *"No."* He then asked if I was willing to put my hand on the Bible and repeat my answer. As I quickly complied, holding onto my lie, I hoped he wouldn't notice my condition.

For years I wrestled with guilt over what I had done that night. Lying was one thing. Putting my hand on the Word of God and lying, in my mind, seemed an unforgivable sin. I felt imprisoned by guilt because of my actions that evening.

It was about 15 years later that I fully understood that the cross was enough to remove the burden of that sin and all the other atrocities I'd ever committed. Still, I knew I had to apologize to my dad. Honestly, I felt a little silly the day I drove to his farm and apologized for something I'd done in my youth. Dad didn't remember the incident at all, but he gladly forgave me. I left there feeling great freedom from the haunting memory of my blatant shortcoming in honesty.

Forgiveness sets prisoners free, while unforgiveness is a felony that can keep us incarcerated under its power. We are all in need of forgiveness from God. As people under his Grace, we are also required to extend forgiveness to others.

Jesus even connected our willingness to forgive with God's forgiveness of us. When teaching the people to pray, He taught them to say: *"And forgive us our debts, as we also have forgiven our debtors* (Matthew. 6:12)."* This begs the question: Have we forgiven others in the way we want God to forgive us?

Many moons ago, after a long hot day at work on a construction site, some coworkers and I swam in a stagnant pond to help cool off. Shortly afterward, I developed a nasty rash that eventually required medical attention. I learned the pond was fed by runoff from surrounding hills. It had no outlet, which meant water flowed in, sat there, and stewed. In the process, the water apparently acquired some very undesirable qualities.

If forgiveness were a healthy pond, it would have both an inlet (a place where it receives) and an outlet (a place where it flows to another body of water). If we try to just receive forgiveness from God and others without giving forgiveness to those who have wronged us, we are a stagnant pond that causes unnecessary unpleasantries both in our lives and the lives of those we refuse to forgive. The rash of unforgiveness will rub us raw as long as we tolerate it. Even worse, it will imprison us and prevent us from experiencing freedom in Christ.

Jesus made this very clear in a parable called the unmerciful servant (Matthew 18:23-35).

In this parable, Jesus talked about a king who wanted to collect a debt from a man who owed him what would be millions in today's currency. The man pleaded for more time, and the king took pity on him and canceled his debt. Imagine the thankfulness this man must have felt!

Recently, at a consignment store holding a sale, some

items caught my eye. I approached the counter with some boxes of mint baseball cards dating back to my teen years along with some other things I was excited to purchase at reduced prices. The problem came when my credit card inexplicably refused to work (I used it earlier that same day and used it again later that day).

I scrambled to figure out what to do since I had no other payment option with me. I told the man in line behind me to go ahead of me while I figured things out. Instead of just paying his own bill, this man told the cashier to add my bill to his total. I was shocked and tried to protest. But he insisted.

This guy's name was Bob. In a brief conversation after the fact, he told me he had recently lost a son. I assured him I would gladly pray for him and his family. Bob taught me about debt forgiveness that day as he paid a price I couldn't.

What joy there is in having a canceled debt, or at least there should be. In His parable, Jesus went on to say that a man owed the forgiven debtor a few thousand dollars. The forgiven man found his debtor, choked him, and demanded his money. The debtor begged for mercy. Instead, the forgiven man had his debtor thrown into prison until he could pay back what was owed. What a nasty man!

It's no wonder that the story emphasizes how servants who witnessed all this went back to the king and squealed on the unforgiving servant. The king summoned the one who'd been forgiven millions and chastised him for his lack of mercy. He threw the merciless man into prison until such time as he could repay the millions he owed.

Then Jesus drops the mic on this teaching by saying: "*So also my heavenly Father will do to every one of you, if you do not forgive your brother from your heart* (Matthew 18:35)."

We might look at this parable and think we have an out. After all, you might say you've never done anything as bad to anyone else as the person needing your forgiveness. You might say God has had to forgive you your thousands while another person needs millions in forgiveness from you. But that would be backwards.

You see, whether our sin is small or great, the wages of that sin is eternal death. The only payment that rescues us from an eternal prison is the gift of Christ Jesus, of life eternal (Romans 6:23). In other words, Jesus has forgiven a debt that was impossible for us. We couldn't pay it back, regardless of how long we might live. In effect, Jesus says, "I've forgiven you for eternity; forgive others who've wronged you temporarily on this earth."

This is a tall order from our Lord. The forgiveness we are asked to give goes beyond our natural ability. It's supernatural. Therefore, we need God's help in doing so. It's one thing to forgive another Christian for talking behind your back or your neighbor for driving his car over your lawn. But there are far worse debts we're asked to forgive. God wants us to extend forgiveness to everyone who has wronged us.

An example of supernatural and miraculous forgiveness comes from the life of Louis Zamperini, a former Olympic star who was fighting in World War II when his plane was shot down. After surviving 47 days at sea, Louis ended up in a Japanese prison camp where he endured horrific conditions. During that time, one of the guards, Mutsuhiro Watanabe (nicknamed "The Bird") tortured Louie relentlessly, getting a charge out of having dominance over an Olympic athlete.

When the war ended, Louis was freed to return home from the prison camp. But in many ways, he was still incarcerated. He was haunted by nightmares of the Bird and the torture he'd been through. Lack of sleep, the stress of transitioning back into society, PTSD from flashbacks, all these played a role in developing his alcohol addiction.

Louis resided in the prison of unforgiveness. Full of hate for his former torturer, Louis made plans to travel to Japan and kill this man so he could be free.

One night in 1949, low on hope and desperate, Louis attended a Billy Graham revival in Los Angeles, where he was living at the time. Louis heard the Gospel message of Jesus Christ, went to the front and surrendered himself to the only one that could handle the demons of his past.

Later in life, Louis testified that, following the night he surrendered to the Savior, he never had a "Bird" nightmare again. Why? Jesus moved to the center of Louis' life. The Bird and thoughts of getting even had to move out.

You see, freedom isn't found in revenge. It's only found in forgiveness at the cross. Knowing he'd been forgiven for the sinful stains in his own life, Louis found the courage to forgive the Bird. Before he could move forward, he had to let go of his *"root of bitterness"* (Hebrews 12:15).

The former Olympic star realized he owed God millions he couldn't repay and was forgiven. He had to extend forgiveness to the Bird for his debt of thousands. It's a story of supernatural forgiveness, Louis needed God's help to get free from the unforgiveness prison. Once that was done, Louis went on to dedicate the rest of his life to serving God by working with troubled youth.†

I've personally come across others who have displayed that level of forgiveness. A man whose son was murdered found the perpetrator in his jail cell. Instead of beating the offender to a bloody pulp, (a natural response), he forgave him (supernatural response).

One inmate, who was active at Living Stone, recognized the man who had abused him in his youth residing in his housing unit at the prison. Instead of unleashing his anger over the brokenness resulting from what this man had done (a natural response), he forgave him (supernatural response).

There are many ways in which a Christ-follower is called to live differently. Forgiveness is one. Don't be housed in a prison of unforgiveness. Be set free. Seek out those who need your forgiveness. Forgive others, so bitterness no longer has its claws in you.

Sometimes that means forgiving people you no longer

---

† I highly recommend the movie "Unbroken, Path to Redemption" (2018 Pure Flix). This is a follow up to the original movie "Unbroken," and highlights Louie's faith journey.

have contact with or who are no longer alive. In such circumstances, I've recommended to inmates that they write a letter to those from whom they need forgiveness or those they need to forgive (even if the letter can't be sent).

Louis tried to meet with the Bird face to face, but it never worked out. For a time, the Bird was thought to be dead. When it was learned he was alive, Louis' torturer refused a meeting. Below is the letter Louis wrote to the Bird instead of meeting with him. It may help guide your thoughts if you need to write something similar.

To Mutsuhiro Watanabe,

As a result of my prisoner of war experience under your unwarranted and unreasonable punishment, my post-war life became a nightmare. It was not so much due to the pain and suffering as it was the tension of stress and humiliation that caused me to hate with a vengeance.

Under your discipline, my rights, not only as a prisoner of war but also as a human being, were stripped from me. It was a struggle to maintain enough dignity and hope to live until the war's end.

The post-war nightmares caused my life to crumble, but thanks to a confrontation with God through the evangelist Billy Graham, I committed my life to Christ. Love has replaced the hate I had for you. Christ said, "Forgive your enemies and pray for them."

As you probably know, I returned to Japan in 1952 and was

graciously allowed to address all the Japanese war criminals
at Sugamo Prison... I asked them about you and was told that
you probably had committed Hara-Kiri, which I was sad to
hear. At that moment, like the others, I also forgave you and
now would hope that you would also become a Christian.
    — *Louis Zamperini*

Reflection Questions

- Why do you think unforgiveness can be such a weight to bear?
- What do you think of the analogy of a stagnant pond being like holding onto unforgiveness?
- Read Matthew 18:23-35. Considering the story, do you believe God has a right to ask us to forgive? Why or why not?
- Did you identify with Louis Zamperini's forgiveness story? Do you have someone you need to ask forgiveness of or offer it to?

*"Freedom is not the right
to do what we want,
but what we ought."*

— *Abraham Lincoln*

14

FREE TO DO
CAPTIVE THINGS?

A few years ago, I found out there was another me. Apparently, the other me had taken a trip to Niagara Falls,† crossed the border into Canada and gotten into trouble and went to jail. At least that's the story he gave over the phone to my now late grandmother, who then sent him thousands of dollars. When Grandma shared the story with my aunt and uncle, who lived in her same Colorado town, they quickly felt an urgent need to investigate what was really going on and discover the truth.

After receiving their phone call, I assured them I had gone nowhere near Canada recently and that the only bars I'd seen were from the outside looking in. The lies were revealed, and the truth came out!

---

† The real me hasn't seen Niagara Falls yet.

Now imagine for a moment that I was an untrustworthy person who would tell the truth straight up one day and then lie flat out the next. When my aunt and uncle needed to get to the bottom of things as far as Grandma and her money were concerned, they wouldn't have been able to take my word for it. They would have had to check with other sources, probably contact authorities to investigate whether or not I had anything to do with it. It would have been a giant mess, and they may never have figured out the truth.

Thankfully, they had reason to believe me because I'd been credible in the past and hadn't stolen anything from anyone for decades. Some dude with no conscience cold-called Grandma and fleeced the saintly woman for a lot of green.†

It was despicable, but the case was closed as far as any wrongdoing on my part was concerned. My aunt and uncle made sure Grandma didn't fall for that sort of trick again.

If you've read this far in this book, you've picked up on the fact that I am a big Bible fan. It's my answer book for life. If I have questions about something, I look to God's Word for guidance to lead me to the truth. If other people have questions for me, I look to God's Word for direction to lead them to the truth.

Unfortunately, many folks, including those attending or even leading churches, have been abandoning the idea that the Bible is our guidebook for faith. Throughout Christian history, it's been taught and believed that God prompted each

---

† When my grandma Harriet learned it was a scam, she began praying for the "other me's" salvation.

human author to write out the stories and teachings of the Old and New Testaments. In other words, the Bible is God-inspired.

As 2 Timothy 3:16-17 puts it: *"All Scripture is breathed out by God and profitable for teaching, for reproof, for correction, and for training in righteousness, that the man of God may be complete, equipped for every good work."*

These two verses clearly describe the role of scripture in the life of a believer. If our goal is to be geared up to do God's work in this world, the pages of scripture will teach, train and correct us as necessary to live in relationship with God and do all the good things God has planned for our lives. But some are taking a different stance on that. They're of the persuasion that God's Word is not inspired. In fact, they treat it as if it is expired.

Recently I got into a brief Facebook debate with another pastor who said, "The Bible was written by man and is not credible." I then questioned that pastor as to what resource they consulted to discover and know the truth. I received no response.

If we treat God's Word like it might be credible about some things, but not others (like the sketchy Jason analogy in the beginning of this chapter), then we can go on a never-ending search for truth and probably never find it.

Thankfully, there is no need for that. What the church needs is men and women with a hunger for the Word. The problems come when people try to make scripture fit their agenda instead of adjusting their lives to the teachings of God's Word.

I look at the heroes of the faith from centuries past, men like Martin Luther. The great theologian said this of the Word: "From the beginning of my Reformation, I have asked God to send me neither dreams, nor visions, nor angels, but to give me the right understanding of His Word, the Holy Scriptures; for as long as I have God's Word, I know that I am walking in His way and that I shall not fall into any error or delusion."

Clearly, this leader of the Protestant Reformation recognized that the path leading away from "error or delusion" was paved with an understanding of God's Word, empowering us to walk in God's ways and keep from falling.

Similarly, the great evangelist Billy Graham said this: "The Bible is God's Word, and if we ignore it, our lives will be morally and spiritually impoverished. Just as we need food and water to grow and be physically healthy, so we need the 'food' and 'water' of God's Word to grow and be spiritually healthy."

If a person thinks the Word is expired and not relevant for our modern-day, we can fully expect that individual will not be in good spiritual health. I recently watched a documentary featuring a pastor who shrugged off a portion of Genesis as a myth.

As I listened to the man, I had no sense at all that the Holy Spirit was directing him. He seemed to be regurgitating information he'd been taught at some point in his ministry training. Nothing he said aligned with the truth of God's Word. It's scary for me to think that this pastor is preaching weekly out of the book of "2nd Opinions."† He's trying to build a spiritual house on a foundation of sand.

John Calvin famously wrote: "A dog barks when his master is attacked. I would be a coward if I saw God's truth is attacked and yet would remain silent." This is something I'm not silent on. I often warn of the dangers of leaving the Word in the dust (or in need of dusting off). We're told in scripture that God's path for us is straight, narrow and sometimes the way will grow dark. That's when we need light the most. Psalm 119:105 says: *"Your Word is a lamp to my feet and a light to my path."*

In this dark and broken world, it is the Word of God that illuminates the path before us so we may walk in the Spirit (Galatians 5:16), on the straight and narrow way leading to life. In my seasons of greatest peace and growth in faith, God's Word leaps off the page and into my life. But Satan and his SWAT team don't want us to believe the truth about the Bible. They work hard to deceive and mislead people about the authority of the Word (2 Corinthians 11:3).

One day a couple years back, Joe, an inmate, and mature believer asked to meet with me. He had a concern about the way something was handled at our most recent communion service. Gripes and preferences are nothing new, but Joe's concern was different. He opened his Bible and read some passages of scripture that supported his stance. Corrected by the Word, I made an adjustment in how we conducted communion

† You'll find that right before the book of "Hesitations."

in the future. I will never be too mature in the faith to be further molded by biblical truth.

If the devil can infiltrate a church and remove from it the application of God's Word; causing followers to merely go through the motions, he will. And he has. Just as a scam artist can act legit while they rob you blind, Satan can masquerade as an angel of light (2 Corinthians 11:14) and point people towards his kingdom instead of God's.

Scripture clearly talks about churches subject to the devil's deception: *"For the time is coming when people will not endure sound teaching, but having itching ears, they will accumulate for themselves teachers to suit their own passions, and will turn away from listening to the truth and wander off into myths* (2 Timothy 4:3–4)."

Many people today are wandering, wondering what the truth might be when God has already given it to us. I don't claim to understand it all. I don't know every nuance in translation from the original Hebrew and Greek into English. But I tell you, when I preach from the Word of God in full confidence that it's the truth, God, through the power of the Holy Spirit, accomplishes things. After all, He was the One who authored the whole thing to begin with.

Whether a person considers the scriptures to be inspired or expired will profoundly affect the impact God's holy book has in their life. If a person buys into the "expired word" theory, they deny themselves a tool that has healing and restoring qualities.

I have worked for a while with Mark, a long-term inmate at Mike Durfee State Prison. His story is quite heartbreaking as his grandfather, a prominent police sergeant in Chicago, severely abused him in his youth. Unfortunately, even though Mark moved away, his grandfather's ways went with him. He became an abuser himself, eventually amassing felonies that will require him to spend a good portion of his life in prison.

Mark doesn't blame his grandfather for his prison sentence. He says justice was done and he must pay for the crimes he committed. Mark was programmed for immorality at a very young age. Now he needs something to which he can cling to that will guide him into truth and rehabilitate his morals.

Thankfully, Mark finds what he needs in scripture, beginning with the message of Salvation through Jesus Christ. He allows the word of God to saturate his life and transform his old patterns of thought. I've lost track of how many times Mark has come to my office and said something like, "I was reading through Hebrews chapter 4 last night, and verse 15† jumped out at me. Let me read it to you, and then I want to hear your take on how that verse applies to my life."

God is using His Word as a tool by which Mark can be corrected and trained in righteousness so he can do good works instead of evil. This isn't the work of an expired piece of ancient literature. This is the work of the living, breathing Word of God!

---

† Hebrews 4:15: "For we do not have a high priest who is unable to sympathize with our weaknesses, but one who in every respect has been tempted as we are, yet without sin." (This is an actual verse we discussed.)

Often the Bible is dismissed because its teachings are considered intolerant in today's society, where tolerance for almost everything (often except for Christian beliefs) is the order of the day. I agree there are many behaviors God's Word tells us are not tolerated by Him. I am utterly convinced that what the world needs is not a faith that cheers us on in our sin. I, for one, needed a faith that called me out of the sins of my youth and still tweaks me in areas I need to surrender further.

If you sincerely study the Bible, it's evident that in some ways the Bible allows for tolerance. I've read and studied scriptures that instruct me to be gentle and respectful to those who don't share my beliefs (1 Peter 3:15), to be patient with those whose faith is weaker (Romans 15:1), and Jesus' challenge, of all things, is for us is to love our enemies (Matthew 5:44). We are called to "play nice" with others when we don't agree with them.

That being said, I believe one of the cruelest things we could ever do is to pretend there is no path of truth. Or to tell people it's ok to remain in sin, expecting perpetual forgiveness while bearing bad fruit. That is clearly not a biblical concept (Matthew 3:8-10; Galatians 5:19-21).

When people ask what Living Stone Prison Church is against, I tell them I prefer to be known as a Pro-New Life in Christ church rather than an anti-anything church. I'd rather be known by what we stand for, not things we stand against.

Some churches say you'll be welcome after you change. Others say you can come in and there's no need for change.

It's always my desire to be part of a church that welcomes people in with an expectation that Jesus will change their lives from the inside out (Colossians 3:1-11).

Finding a good church can be a very tricky thing, especially since opinions of what defines a good church vary greatly. The whole denomination thing is very confusing for someone with no background in Christianity.†

During a recent visit to South Dakota's Pine Ridge Indian Reservation, my friend Dale and I met up with Travis, a former member of our congregation. Travis introduced us to some people on the "Rez" who are involved in ministering to Native Americans there.

Afterward, Travis began sharing about his struggle to find a church when he first became a believer. He thought all churches were the same. After all, they all talk and sing about the same Jesus . . . right? But in churches in his area, he found a lot of quarreling. In fact, one pastor told him not to go to this church, another told him not to go to that church. Unsure of what to do, Travis wandered from one church to another until he found one where he felt the unmistakable presence of God. It became his consistent house of worship.

I am "ecumenical" in my thinking, which means I gladly work with other believers who belong to a different denomination, provided their beliefs are biblical. There are, however, many spiritually dead churches out there. Perhaps you are

---

† Let's be honest, denominations can also be very confusing for those of us who've attended church for decades.

reading this, and wondering if it's time to find a new place to worship.

Or perhaps you've never attended a church, and you're wondering what to look for in a worshiping body of believers. I've also counseled many a man as they prepared to leave prison and look for a place to plug in, and continue their journey of following Jesus. It's vitally important to our faith journey that we're involved with a church that promotes the truth.

Here are some things I consider non-negotiable in a church I belong to:

- A recognition of God the Father, Son and Holy Spirit and the Bible's explanation of their roles as Creator, Savior, Sustainer, etc. (Genesis 1:1; John 3:16; Romans 8:11).

- A recognition that Jesus is who He says He is, the Way, the truth, the Life, the only way to God the Father and His Kingdom (John 14:6).

- A place where the sacraments (communion/baptism) are practiced responsibly and are not presented as a way in which we are saved, but as visible ways in which we experience Grace and celebrate and understand Salvation in Jesus Christ alone (Matthew 28:19; Luke 22:19-20).

- A place that recognizes the Word of God as inspired and relevant for today, which means preaching both Grace and repentance (Hebrews 4:12; 2 Timothy 3:16-17; Matthew 4:4).

- A group of believers doing the will of God and active in

ministering to its community and the world in general, not just talking about it (James 1:22-24; 2:14-17).

If those factors are in place, I'd be willing to bet you've found a church body that is alive. There are other fine points of theology that are important, but the above list will give you a reliable place to start. There are also things to consider, such as traditional hymns or contemporary music, preaching styles, etc. Those are matters of personal preference. The main thing is to find a place where there's life, and you are spiritually fed, then let God take it from there.

When an inmate is released from prison, he or she can go back to the practices that led to incarceration in the first place, or they can embrace a new life. Often, I've heard a "short-timer" (an inmate close to leaving) say, "When I get out, I need a new playground and new playmates."† In other words, they need to change out the areas in which they live and the people they hang around, or they will likely return to prison.

There's something to be learned from that for anyone who has found freedom in Christ. If we hang around in the same places we did before with the same people we will most likely find ourselves doing "captive things" once again. We need a new playground and new playmates.

One key to persevering in faith is to find a vibrant Bible-believing church that will challenge and encourage you in

---

†   There can come a day when a person is strong in faith and ready to be a light to their "old playground."

your faith. If you don't have one that fits that description, I hope and pray that you find one soon.

Reflection Questions

- Read 2 Timothy 3:1-7. What does it look like when a church has a form of godliness but denies God's power?
- What are some ways you think Satan leads churches astray in today's society?
- What are some views you've heard about the reliability of the Bible? Where did those views come from?
- Why do you think some churches reject the fact that the Bible is inspired? Where then do you think such churches go to find truth?
- Read 2 Timothy 3:16-17. What do these verses reveal about the importance of scripture?

*"The most pathetic person
in the world is someone
who has sight but
has no vision."*

— Helen Keller

15

VISIONS OF
FREEDOM

A while back, I was asked to do a little speaking at a charity auction. Organizers weren't looking for a sermon, just a few words here and there to get the audience in the check-writing mood.

I decided to open with a joke I'd come across about wolf hunting in Idaho. Just for fun, I used my friend Greg and his twin brothers as the main characters. Greg was at the auction, too.

In telling the joke, I made an error. I hadn't considered that most people there didn't know Greg and didn't realize I was making up his role in my story. So the crowd bought into the far-fetched tale about him and his brothers wolf hunting to bag a hefty bounty. They thought my story was true.

The punchline comes when the trio is surrounded by growling, hungry wolves as they sleep. I explained how Greg woke up, groggily rubbed his eyes, looked at their predicament and declared, "Boys! We're rich!"†

No one laughed. It was the funny part, but most of the audience was still waiting for me to finish the engaging story. They completely missed the point!!!

I really hope you don't miss the point of this book. If you've been reading it cover to cover and thinking to yourself, "Jason is super spiritual and has all the answers," you'd be super spiritually wrong. My story is that of an average Joe (or as I felt for much of my life, an under-average Joe) whom God called out of many self-imposed prisons to minister to others living in their own literal and figurative prisons.

I certainly don't have all the answers to life's many issues. But I know Who does.

From where I sit today, I understand why God most often chose men like shepherds and fisherman to do his bidding. Men like that know they can't do it on their own, so they're less apt to try and more likely to listen to God's instructions.

In my younger years, I had multiple people ask me how I knew the claims of the Bible and of Christianity were true. I remember responding with wishy-washy answers, pointing toward obvious arguments like the world had to come from somewhere, our country was founded on Christian values and it took off, (etc.).

Now, I can say my faith is built on the cross of Jesus Christ

---

† Get it? Their lives were in grave danger and all he saw were $$$$$$. Please say you get it!

and amplified by the fact that God has been consistently and purposely carrying out His plan for my life from the very beginning. There have been periods when I was oblivious to how He was working in my life. Only as I look back do I recognize His ongoing agenda.

There hasn't been a season when He wasn't faithful, no triumph or tribulation that wasn't used somehow for His glory and my own good (Romans 8:28), even if I didn't see that at the time.

As I look ahead to what's in store, I don't know where God is taking my story from here. I do know Jesus says not to worry about our future but planning for it is not off-limits.

When Jarrod left Mike Durfee State Prison a few months ago, his heart was in good spiritual condition. He had an excellent parole plan and found a suitable church right away. Jarrod did very well on the outside for several months. However, he eventually became severely stressed while trying to assist other struggling former inmates.

Jarrod started using substances to ease his stress, which led to a full-blown slide back into his addiction and a free trip back to prison.

Jarrod knows full well the whole episode could have been avoided. He acknowledges he was unprepared for the distress of feeling like he failed to help others.

In Jarrod's case, he had a plan and a vision for life on the outside. His blind spot kept him from anticipating unforeseen stressors. He knows there's work to do to prepare himself for his next opportunity to live successfully outside the razor wire fence. He knows he'll need to keep his focus on Jesus when trials present themselves.

Jesus once said this to his followers: *"In the world, you will have tribulation. But take heart; I have overcome the world* (John 16:33b)." I love that promise because I don't know what life might throw my way—good, bad, or otherwise. I don't know what "prison" may attempt to confine me in the future.

I do know Jesus has overcome it all. That tells me that whatever I'm going through, I can maintain hope through it all because my Savior has it covered. That truth, applied to Jarrod's life, could have kept him out of prison.

In past chapters, we looked at several different types of prisons where we can do time. I don't want to go back into my former captivity. I'm sure you don't want to either.

Avoiding self-made prisons requires vision, especially since we don't know what we'll face in the future. But God does, which is why we need His vision going forward.

Proverbs 29:18 says: *"Where there is no prophetic vision the people cast off restraint, but blessed is he who keeps the law."* A prophetic vision is a vision from God, His vision for our life and future. Without it, we run amok with worry and try and to take matters into our own hands.

God has made some reliable promises which, once we trust in them, give us the ability to successfully abide with Him in both sunshine and rain.

As a kid, I remember singing beautiful old hymns of faith

in church.†

One of them included this verse;

Standing on the promises, I cannot fail.
Listening every moment to the Spirit's call,
Resting in my Savior as my all in all,
Standing on the promises of God.

(*Standing on the Promises* by Russell Kelso Carter)

Those are some challenging lyrics to live out, but they also provide a prophetic vision of what God can do in our lives through the good, the bad, and the ugly. These words are promises straight out of the Bible. As God's children, we can embrace them.

God has offered us everything we need to live for Him both now and forever. We cannot dictate how Satan will try to imprison us and cause our faith to be ineffective. We CAN decide, before pitfalls appear, to stubbornly follow Jesus through it all. In a nutshell, that's God's prophetic vision for our life.

I love this quote from C.S. Lewis: "I believe in Christianity as I believe that the sun has risen: not only because I see it, but because by it, I see everything else."

I am thankful to God that my faith has become something that bubbles over in me so that I have to share it. I praise God that He's delivered me from my dark and cold prison cells and into His freedom. Already He's stamped my life with purpose, and I look to Him expectantly into the future.

---

†   I might have sung them like a donkey with strep throat, but the words were still beautiful.

How about you, my friend? I don't know what prisons (literal or figurative) you've spent time in during your past. You may be in one (literal or figurative) right now.

The "prison paradox" (a statement that defies common sense) is that when a person finds themselves stuck, imprisoned by physical bars or by circumstances of life, there is great opportunity for good to come from it. When we invite Jesus into our brokenness, our life's journey becomes an overcomer's story in which God gets the glory. We all need to hear such stories. Our journey through brokenness in the past can become part of someone else's survival guide for their present.

My hope and prayer for you is that the stories and scriptural insight in this book have encouraged you to move forward in the freedom that Jesus Christ has earned for you.

Closing Prayer:
Lord God, I pray for revival for the one holding this book. I ask that you reveal to us any area of our lives in which we are still imprisoned and give us the power and perseverance to grasp and hold onto the freedom You offer. Whether it's the freedom of the cross over sin or freedom from whatever is limiting our effectiveness. I pray we find the key that opens the gate to the abundant life You came to earth to offer us.

In Jesus' name,

Amen

Reflection Questions

- What distinctions do you think we can make between a personal vision and God's prophetic vision?

- This is a conversation Billy Graham often shared: "If Christianity is valid, why is there so much evil in the world?" To this question, the famous preacher replied, "With so much soap, why are there so many dirty people in the world? Christianity, like soap, must be personally applied if it is to make a difference in our lives." Does Billy's response make sense to you? Why or why not?

- Read 2 Corinthians 1:20. Do you find it hard to accept the biblical truth found in the lyrics of *Standing on the Promises?* What do you think it would take for you to be able to sing that song with all your heart?

- Read John 16:33. These were words Jesus said just before going to the cross. Why do you think it was vital for him to encourage the disciples for what was ahead? "I have overcome the world"? What encouragement do you find in those words?

ACKNOWLEDGMENTS

Special thanks to my wife for encouraging me to write this book and for steady support in the crazy journey.

Thank you to my mom for your constant and prayerful presence in my life and in ministry.

To all the individuals who ran the ministry for two months while we were on sabbatical (Dennis and Connie, Stan, Elroy, Jeff and the roster of gifted preachers who filled the pulpit) thank you for all your help.

To my editor, Loretta, thank you for giving me confidence in the process.

Thanks to Jennifer for providing the foreword and to Chris, Mike and Nick for helping me choose my words wisely.

Thank you to Lisa and Travis for contributing your drawings.

Thank you to the staff of the prison systems of South Dakota for allowing us the freedom to do our work.

Special thanks to the many individuals, both in and out of the prison, who have allowed me to share a piece of their story.

Above all, thank you, Jesus. Indeed, in Your will, all things are possible.

"You can accomplish one thousand times more by resting in Jesus than working for Him."

—Pastor Quincy Afraid of Lightning

REFERENCES

Attacking Anxiety and Depression. (2003). Oak Harbor, OH: Midwest Center for Stress and Anxiety.

Hillenbrand, L. (2010). *Unbroken.* New York, NY: Random House Trade.

Logan, J. (1995). *Reclaiming Surrendered Ground.* Chicago, IL: Moody Publishers.

Lusko, L. (2018). *I Declare War.* Nashville, TN: W Publishing.

Ramundo, K. K. (1993, 2006). *You Mean I'm Not Lazy, Stupid or Crazy?!* New York, NY: Scribner.

Sphere, D. (2005). *Cain's Redemption.* Chicago, IL: Northfield.

CONTACT US
(or to order more books)

Website: www.psalm40publishing.com
Facebook: Prison Paradox
Or write us: Prison Paradox, PO Box 23, Canton, SD 57103

ABOUT THE AUTHOR

Jason grew up in rural Northwest Iowa. He describes his childhood community as very tight-knit and somewhat sheltered.

However, God prepared and sent him into South Dakota's prison system among diverse people where he has learned much about the brokenness of the world and the power of God's Grace. In 2011, along with his wife Ruth, Jason planted the Living Stone Prison Church in the Mike Durfee State Prison in Springfield, South Dakota. He has pastored this congregation since its birth.

Jason enjoys spending time outdoors, especially with his family. He has a strong sense of adventure and loves to see and explore areas of the United States and the world where he's never been.

Most of all, Jason's greatest desire is to witness how Jesus continues to save, heal, and deliver people from the power of darkness.

CPSIA information can be obtained
at www.ICGtesting.com
Printed in the USA
FSHW012331110421
80264FS

9 780578 545943